# *the* dance

# *the* *dance*

**ORIAH MOUNTAIN DREAMER**

Thorsons

Thorsons
An Imprint of HarperCollins*Publishers*
77–85 Fulham Palace Road,
Hammersmith, London W6 8JB

and *Thorsons*
are trademarks of
HarperCollins*Publishers* Limited

The Thorsons website address is: www.thorsons.com

First published by HarperCollins Publishers, Inc., NY
This edition published by Thorsons 2002

1 3 5 7 9 10 8 6 4 2

A catalogue record of this book
is available from the British Library

ISBN 0 00 711299 8

Designed by Joseph Rutt

Printed and bound in Great Britain by
Clays Ltd, St Ives plc, Bungay, Suffolk

For Linda Mulhall
for all the years of dancing as best friends

There are lovers content with longing
I'm not one of them.

*Rumi (trans. Coleman Barks)*

# CONTENTS

## Prelude

*What if it truly doesn't matter what you do but how you do whatever you do?*

*How would this change what you choose to do with your life?*

*What if you could be more present and openhearted with each person you met if you were working as a cashier in a corner store, or as a parking lot attendant, than you could if you were doing a job you think is more important?*

*How would this change how you want to spend your precious time on this earth?*

*What if your contribution to the world and the fulfillment of your own happiness is not dependent upon discovering a better method of prayer or technique of meditation, not dependent upon reading the right book or attending the right seminar, but upon really seeing and deeply appreciating yourself and the world as they are right now?*

*How would this affect your search for spiritual development?*

*What if there is no need to change, no need to try to transform yourself into someone who is more compassionate, more present, more loving or wise?*

*How would this affect all the places in your life where you are endlessly trying to be better?*

*What if the task is simply to unfold, to become who you already are in your essential nature—gentle, compassionate, and capable of living fully and passionately present?*

*How would this affect how you feel when you wake up in the morning?*

*What if who you essentially are right now is all that you are ever going to be?*

*How would this affect how you feel about your future?*

*What if the essence of who you are and always have been is enough?*

*How would this affect how you see and feel about your past?*

*What if the question is not why am I so infrequently the person I really want to be, but why do I so infrequently want to be the person I really am?*

*How would this change what you think you have to learn?*

*What if becoming who and what we truly are happens not through striving and trying but by recognizing and receiving the people and places and practices that offer us the warmth of encouragement we need to unfold?*

*How would this shape the choices you make about how to spend today?*

*What if you knew that the impulse to move in a way that creates beauty in the world will arise from deep within and guide you every time you simply pay attention and wait?*

*How would this shape your stillness, your movement, your willingness to follow this impulse, to just let go and dance?*

## The Dance

I have sent you my invitation,
the note inscribed on the palm of my hand by the fire of living.
Don't jump up and shout, "Yes, this is what I want! Let's do it!"
Just stand up quietly and dance with me.

Show me how you follow your deepest desires,
spiraling down into the ache within the ache,
and I will show you how I reach inward and open outward
to feel the kiss of the Mystery, sweet lips on my own, every day.

Don't tell me you want to hold the whole world in your heart.
Show me how you turn away from making another wrong without
abandoning yourself when you are hurt and afraid of being unloved.

Tell me a story of who you are,
and see who I am in the stories I am living.
And together we will remember that each of us always has a choice.

Don't tell me how wonderful things will be . . . someday.
Show me you can risk being completely at peace,
truly okay with the way things are right now in this moment,
and again in the next and the next and the next . . .

I have heard enough warrior stories of heroic daring.
Tell me how you crumble when you hit the wall,
the place you cannot go beyond by the strength of your own will.

*What carries you to the other side of that wall,*
*to the fragile beauty of your own humanness?*

*And after we have shown each other how we have set and kept the*
*clear, healthy boundaries that help us live side by side with each other,*
*let us risk remembering that we never stop silently loving*
*those we once loved out loud.*

*Take me to the places on the earth that teach you how to dance,*
*the places where you can risk letting the world break your heart,*
*and I will take you to the places where the earth beneath my feet*
*and the stars overhead make my heart whole again and again.*

*Show me how you take care of business*
*without letting business determine who you are.*
*When the children are fed but still the voices within and around us*
*shout that soul's desires have too high a price,*
*let us remind each other that it is never about the money.*

*Show me how you offer to your people and the world*
*the stories and the songs you want our children's children to remember,*
*and I will show you how I struggle,*
*not to change the world, but to love it.*

*Sit beside me in long moments of shared solitude,*
*knowing both our absolute aloneness and our undeniable belonging.*
*Dance with me in the silence and in the sound of small daily words,*
*holding neither against me at the end of the day.*

*And when the sound of all the declarations of our sincerest*
*intentions has died away on the wind,*
*dance with me in the infinite pause before the next great inhale*
*of the breath that is breathing us all into being,*
*not filling the emptiness from the outside or from within.*

*Don't say, "Yes!"*
*Just take my hand and dance with me.*

ORIAH MOUNTAIN DREAMER

# ONE

# *But Can You Dance?*

*I have sent you my invitation,*
*the note inscribed on the palm of my hand by the fire of living.*
*Don't jump up and shout, "Yes, this is what I want! Let's do it!"*
*Just stand up quietly and dance with me.*

The advantage of the written word is that I can tell you here near the beginning what was only revealed to me near the end: I write these words to name myself—to name each of us—worthy of going home, worthy of having our longing met, worthy of awakening in the arms of the Beloved. Finding and voicing our soul's longing is not enough. Our ability to live in a way that is consistent with our longing—our ability to dance—is dependent upon what we believe we must do. If our intention is to change who we essentially are, we will fail. If our intention is to become who we essentially are, we cannot help but live true to the deepest longings of our soul.

It is a shining autumn day, the kind of day when the blue of the sky startles you into believing that all things are possible. I'm standing in the quad, a tree-filled green space between the old stone buildings of St. Michael's College at the University of Toronto. But I am not aware of the warm sun or the cool breeze or the students laughing and talking and being vibrantly twenty years old on the lawn. All I can hear is my forty-four-year-old heart thundering in my ears, pounding so hard and fast that my body quakes with the reverberations. Each time I take a step, sweat trickles down the sides of my rib cage beneath my wool sweater. Long, thin pains radiate out from my chest and down both arms like shards of glass making their way along my arteries. A giant hand is tearing my heart out of my chest, and I am afraid.

It probably tells you more than I want you to know about me that it never crosses my mind to ask any of those passing by for help. Stoic to what I am suddenly afraid might be the end, I think to myself, "Oriah, this would be a very stupid place to die." Later I wonder what a smart place to die would look like, but for the moment I focus on moving forward, convinced that I will be all right if I can make it to the library just across the quad and lie down in one of the large armchairs in the reading room.

And then suddenly, there on the sidewalk beneath the sun of an impossibly ordinary afternoon, I hear part of the Pablo Neruda poem "Keeping Quiet" running through my head like the lyrics to some sad melody being played in my body:

*If we were not so single-minded*
*about keeping our lives moving,*
*and for once could do nothing,*
*perhaps a huge silence*
*might interrupt this sadness*
*of never understanding ourselves*
*and of threatening ourselves with death.*

I am aware of what feels like a sharp, desert-dry stone in my throat. I swallow it and focus on taking another step. It takes me ten minutes to traverse the usual two-minute walk to the library. Lying in a lounge chair, I feel the pain slowly abate as my heartbeat gradually returns to normal. And the last line of Neruda's poem runs through my mind again and again. Why am I threatening myself with death? One doctor later declares I have had a mild heart attack, while another maintains it was severe angina. Either way the message is the same: despite the articulation of my sincerest intention to slow down and rest, I continue to do too much, to run too fast, to try too hard. I continue to threaten myself with death.

And this—this refusal to rest—is not the only way in which I have been failing to live consistent with my deepest desire to be fully present with myself and others. Lying there in the library reviewing the last few months of my life, I am aware of a gap I fear is an abyss between my longing to live passionately and intimately with myself and others and the choices I continue to make, the ways in which I fail to love myself or others well.

I'd failed to see the signs of advanced alcoholism and severe depression in the man who had come into my life the previous spring. Although he functioned reasonably well during the day as an architect, I eventually learned that Paul kept a nightly ritual of consuming large volumes of Scotch. It was a pain-numbing habit he'd developed five years earlier after his wife had died in a car crash when he'd fallen asleep at the wheel. Had I heard all of what Paul had told me from the beginning—that despite his desire to rebuild his life he did not think he could ever love or be loved again, that he was winding down toward death—would I still have loved him? I believe I would have. I'd seen the tender heart, fine mind, and gentle spirit beneath the pain and the addiction. But had I seen and accepted the choices he was making for his life—for his death—I would have loved him as I do now, from a distance, not hoping for a relationship of deep intimacy and partnership. When I walked away full of sadness for what could have been, I thought to myself, "I should have told him from the beginning, 'It doesn't interest me if your answer to my invitation is "Yes!" I want to know if you can dance.'" But the truth was that he had told me from the start that he couldn't. I just hadn't wanted to hear it. Counseling hundreds of women over the past fifteen years, I have come to believe that most men tell the truth at the outset of a relationship, even when—or perhaps particularly when—the women they are speaking to are practicing selective listening, are not able or willing to be fully present with what is.

But nowhere had I failed to be present in the way I wanted to be as I had with my elder son, Brendan.

Brendan's father and I discover in the spring that he has once again been lying to us about attending school. And when someone you love lies to you it can break your heart to know that they do not trust that you will love them if the truth is told. Smart, caring, and confused, Brendan is clearly unhappy, unable to decide what he wants to do and unwilling to take advice or seek guidance. Nothing too abnormal for a nineteen-year-old. And I, a completely normal mother of a confused nineteen-year-old, am torturing myself with images of him living in my basement and sleeping until noon at the age of forty-five. I am alternately furious with him and sick with worry that he will not find a way into his own happiness. I want to be patient and caring and supportive. More often I am frantic, critical, and nagging. Our love for each other is never in doubt, but our ability to be in the same room together without conflict is. The arguments are frequent, heated, and increasingly nasty, wearing us both out and leaving me heartsick.

I know I need to trust Brendan to make his own choices and take the consequences, but I am afraid for him. Writing and meditating alone at a wilderness retreat at the end of a long summer of conflict, I resolve to do things differently: I will be more patient; he's only nineteen, he has time to make choices. I will worry less; after all he's not drinking or taking drugs. I will be more supportive—silent about his mistakes, applauding his successes. I'm not naive. I know it will be difficult, but I have hope that the strength of my longing to love him well will guide me in being a better mother. I can honestly say there is nothing I want more in my life. Maybe this is what makes parenting so hard—it matters too much. My human mistakes, my errors in judgment, my lack of wisdom are hardest to accept here where I am deeply attached to the outcome.

Full of heartfelt intentions to do better, I arrive home from my time alone to find Brendan waiting for me in the living room of our home. Two weeks earlier he had agreed that while I was away he would see a counselor, consider his options, make some decisions, and take some actions—getting admission information for schools, applying for jobs, talking to his father. And in two weeks, after an entire summer of doing absolutely nothing, he has done none of it—no thinking, no deciding, no acting.

And in ninety seconds all the resolve I had to be calm and patient and supportive evaporates. I am not exaggerating. Ninety seconds is all it takes.

"You did nothing?" My voice slides up an octave with all the ease if not the sweetness of an operatic soprano. "Nothing? You promised. I let you take your time. What were you thinking would happen when

I came back? I can't believe this!" I question, plead, and accuse and then collapse into silence, more devastated by my reaction than his continued inaction, all hope drained from my body and heart. I've failed him. I've failed myself. Admitting defeat and afraid of inflicting more damage, I do the only thing I can think of. I tell him to move out, to go to his father's. It is not a plan. It is not a strategy. It is a desperate attempt to shift things, if not for him then at least between us. Grief splits me open, but I know we cannot continue as we are.

Brendan moves to his father's that day. Two days later he applies for a job and starts working at the end of the week, flipping burgers at a local fast-food place. As I write this nine months later he is still working, putting money aside, sorting out what he wants to do but clearly happier than he was nine months ago. He comes over frequently, but the new distance between us—albeit small as his father lives eight doors away—is helping us learn a new way of being together. I catch myself before I tell him that he needs a shave, should wear a warmer sweater, or shouldn't be drinking caffeine—well, at least half the time. And the other half of the time he generously ignores me.

With my heart bruised by all three of these failures to live my desire to love myself and others well, it becomes painfully obvious to me that the intention to live consistent with soul-felt desires is not enough even when those desires are deeply felt and clearly articulated. *I want to know why I am so infrequently the person I really want to be.* So I start writing, because writing is my way of searching, of opening to possible wisdom. I'm not interested in why I don't act on intentions that don't really matter to me. I know why I don't exercise even though I repeatedly declare I will: I don't like exercise; I don't actually want to exercise; it's something I think I should do, not something I fully intend to do. But I do want to know why I repeatedly fail to live the intentions that matter to me. I want to know how to narrow the gap between the sincerest desires of my soul and my daily actions. I believe that being willing to be with the truth about myself is the necessary first step in narrowing the gap between my intentions and my actions. And I'm right. I just can't imagine or anticipate what that truth is and what it will require of me.

One night, after several months of writing, one of the elders who has appeared in my dreams for over fifteen years, one of those I call the Grandmothers, comes and speaks to me while I sleep. "Wrong question, Oriah," she says. *"The question is not why are you so infrequently the people you really want to be. The question is why do you so infrequently want to be the people you really are."* She pauses. "Because you have no faith that who you are is enough." Her voice is soft, full of sadness. "But it is. Your true nature as human beings is compassionate, and this essential nature makes you capable of being intimately and fully present. Who you really are is enough."

I wake up, flip on the light, and write in my journal—*The question is not why are we so infrequently the people we really want to be. The question is why do we so infrequently want to be the people we really are.* Sitting in my bed in the predawn light, I am stunned into a strange stillness. The pen falls from my hand, and the journal lies open on my lap. For perhaps the first and possibly the last time in my life, thought is impossible. The silence around and within me grows like the palpable, extended quiet that comes after the sound of a great bell has faded to nothing. Later I will question and doubt and complain that it would have been nice if this course correction had been offered sometime before I had written seven whole chapters. But there will never be any erasing the knowledge I have in that moment that what the

Grandmother is telling me is true: that who we are by our essential nature is enough; that we are right now in this moment capable of being compassionate and fully present in intimate relationship with ourselves, the world, and the Mystery; that we are all we need to be by our nature; that there is no need for self-improvement; that we live our deepest soul's desires not by intending to *change* who we are but by intending to *be* who we are. And clearly our intention—to change or to be who we are—profoundly shapes how we live, what we believe we must do to learn, whether we feel we must ceaselessly push ourselves to reach higher or simply find the courage and confidence to allow who we are to unfold. The latter view calls for choices that support and expand our essentially compassionate nature, while the former aims to reshape our essentially flawed nature with heroic efforts of endless trying.

Despite the fact that endless trying isn't working, it's what I know. It's hard to believe that I can be enough as I am. I want to be *more*— *more* compassionate, *more* present, *more* conscious and aware, *more* loved and loving, *more* intimate with myself and the world. I want to know how to be different—better—than I am. Even though I have failed to consistently live my deepest desires and am exhausted by the endless effort to become who I think I will have to be to live these desires, I resist letting go of the trying. I trust my ability to work hard. I have no experience with or faith in my ability to simply be.

This lack of faith in who we are is embedded in the bones of the culture we have created. We are surrounded by the assumption of our innate inadequacy, the notion of original sin made implicit in a secular culture preaching achievement, improvement, and change. The marketplace is flooded with books and tapes and speakers telling us how to change and transform ourselves into something other than what we are, implicitly telling us that who we really are is not enough, is at best deeply flawed and weak and at worst nasty and aggressive. In a word: sinful.

Many of the New Age spiritual teachers talk a great deal about how our consciousness is "evolving." Now this may or may not be true, although I think you could argue that becoming more efficient producers of weapons of mass destruction and relying more and more exclusively on our rational thinking to the exclusion or undervaluing of our emotions and intuition could be seen as evidence of some devolution. But even if you choose to believe that we are evolving—and it would be an amazingly arrogant species-centric assumption even for us to say that the process somehow stopped with the magnificence of Homo sapiens—anyone who has studied the process of evolution will tell you that it is very, very slow and therefore unlikely to be of any real assistance to me in my quest to become a more patient and loving mother before my sons reach retirement. Calling upon evolution as the hoped-for salvation and making suggestions that seem to indicate that we can somehow make it happen faster if we try harder says that our very nature needs to be fundamentally transformed in order for us to be the people we really want to be.

Secular preachers put forward a similar idea in a different guise. I recently sat in on a presentation given to corporate coaches, folks who work with displaced CEOs and corporate executives. The presenter, a bright and entertaining motivational speaker, was not talking about increasing profits or acquiring more material possessions. In fact, he was questioning the usefulness of these goals in our lives and talking instead about living more fully every day, an intention that echoed my own. But as he urged his audience with real evangelical zeal to "go the extra mile" in living more fully, to become better parents, better coaches, better executives, to get up an hour early to exercise, to get up two hours early to meditate *and* exercise, to take someone new to lunch every week . . . I could feel myself becoming exhausted just listening to him. And as I looked at the quiet, tired faces of the men and women in the audience—men and women already running on too little sleep and too much caffeine—I felt an insurmountable heaviness in my limbs. I could feel myself agreeing with him: yes, these were all the things I would have to do to be consistent with my intention to live fully. And I knew right then and there that I was not going to make it, that I would never be good enough or disciplined enough to do all the things I would have to do to consistently live my soul's longings or this man's aspirations. I simply didn't have within me the energy to make all the necessary incremental upgrades.

Weary and discouraged, I was contemplating returning to the free breakfast buffet for another high-fat croissant—what the hell, I was never going to do half of what I should anyway, so why not?—when the speaker said something that woke me up. With absolute conviction he said, "The harder you are on yourself, the easier life will be on you!" Something inside me snapped awake. I *knew* this was wrong. He was offering a deal: if you drive yourself, life will reward you. And in a flash I knew that this was the place I would land over and over again, driving my body and heart to the point of exhaustion in the hopes of the ever-elusive inner spiritual makeover, if I thought the central question was *why are we so infrequently the people we really want to be?* And if success is at best unlikely, the only hope is a deal, a magic formula that offers a promise and keeps us on the treadmill of self-improvement in the hopes that someone or something will see our effort and grant us a boon.

Still, some days—my sons might say weeks—searching for evidence that my essential nature is compassionate would be pretty slim pickings. Sometimes I'm a shit. Really. I automatically judge as flaky people who use names like Ophelia Morning Glory, which is pretty cheeky for a woman who writes and speaks under the name Oriah Mountain Dreamer. I spend too much time picking at my sons for little things like not wrapping the cheese up tight enough so the edges won't get dark and hard and forgetting to feed the cat. I suspect them of deliberately leaving their oversized sneakers in the hallway where I am sure to trip over them. I get angry at people who don't do things my way, like the young woman on the phone who sounds like she is twelve and will not let me send my courier shipment collect to my publisher, even though I have done it a dozen times before, because it has just dawned on her that the United States is a different country from Canada and the company policy is that you cannot make collect international shipments. And, believe me, I can get pretty nasty when someone who is just doing their job or having a bad day cannot see that My Way is better.

But then I think of those I love. In contrast to the way I see myself, I have little difficulty thinking of others I know as being basically, essentially good even while I can see aspects of them that are less endearing. Linda, who has been my best friend for twenty-two years, has a temper, and even though she was once a Catholic nun (or perhaps because of it), she can swear like a trooper when she is angry. Even though I don't actually believe in hell, I have upon occasion thought to myself, when hearing a string of epithets come from her mouth that would make a sailor blush, "Well, we're all going to hell just for hearing that one!"

Lately Linda has been going through some major changes in her life. If you met her at the moment you might think she is basically a very angry woman, and if you told me this I would tell you without hesitation that Linda is just very frightened right now. Linda's fear comes out as anger. I do not have any problem keeping sight of the fact that Linda is not her anger, that Linda in some essential and basic way is a gentle, compassionate woman truly capable of being fully present and loving with anyone on the planet. How do I know this? Because I have seen it. Now of course you could point out that I have also seen the impatience and the anger. So why do I not feel the least bit confused about which is the essential Linda? I don't know. I just *know* that who she *really* is is the good stuff. Love is what lets me see this in Linda and know that it is true. Clearly this may be the perspective I am missing when examining myself.

But if humans by their essential nature are basically compassionate and capable of being fully present, why then do we so often act out of anger or harshness or distraction? Again, when I look at someone I love, the answer to this question is not such a mystery. Fear. Linda behaves in a way that is inconsistent with her basic compassionate nature when she is afraid, when fear comes between her and her knowledge of who and what she is, knowledge that would reassure her that she belongs in some fundamental way, that who she is is made of the same stuff as I am and you are and the world is so that no real harm can come to her essential self.

It is the same for each of us, although what makes us afraid—what makes us forget who and what we are—may be different. There are many ways to describe the factors that shape our fear and influence our behavior: past trauma and conditioning, inherited tendencies and learned responses, past-life karma, and current pressures, human biology, psychology, and spirituality. We can develop some useful self-understanding by considering any or all of these, but I do not believe we can ever claim to have a definitive explanation for all of our behavior. We remain, like so much of the universe, something of a mystery to ourselves. Whatever the reasons for behavior that is inconsistent with the basic compassionate nature the Grandmother claims we are, the useful question if we want to live our soul's longing is, How can we expand the opportunities and increase the probabilities of living consistent with this nature? How can we dance?

If I want to live my ability to be fully present and compassionate, my ability to be with it all—the joy and the sorrow—I must find the ways, the people, the places, the practices that support me in being all I truly am. I must cultivate ways of being that let me feel the warmth of encouragement against my heart when it is weary. I must be fiercely and compassionately honest with myself about those choices and actions that are inconsistent with my deepest nature and soul's desires. I must find the song lines that run through my life, the melodies that remind me of what I really am and call me gently back to acting on this knowing. I must learn how to dance.

*The Dance* is about finding ways to let our essential nature guide our choices and our actions. It's about honestly looking at the times when it is hard for us to remember and be guided by who we really are—the times when we are tired and hurt, frightened and angry. It's about the places in this culture where it is easy to become confused about who we are—when we are dealing with money and sex and death and power.

Loudly declaring our soul's desires can get the blood running and our passions blazing. When I shared a prose poem I had written declaring my soul's longing with men and women who had done workshops and retreats with me, many responded with a sincere "Yes!" to the call they heard to live more fully present in their lives and in the world. I heard stories from men and women who told me that they had used the prose poem as a litmus test for choosing mates. One woman told me that on her third date with a new man in her life, she had read the piece aloud and waited to see his reaction. When he took her hands in his, looked into her eyes, and said enthusiastically, "I want you to know I say 'Yes!' to all of it," she felt she knew this was the man for her. Another young woman introduced me to her fiancé, the man who had responded enthusiastically to the poem months before, after her boyfriend at the time had shrugged indifferently to the piece.

I love hearing these stories, and heaven only knows I and others have gotten together with potential mates on flimsier evidence than mutual enthusiasm for writing we find meaningful. I will admit I wonder if asking someone who is obviously interested in getting to know you in the biblical sense what they think of a poem you clearly feel is important is likely to elicit anything but a positive and enthusiastic response, but I am not cynical about good intentions. Voicing our intentions is often part of becoming clear about and making a commitment to action. Sometimes, when these intentions are voiced in words that come from the deepest parts of ourselves in moments of clarity about what really matters, the words themselves have the power to open our hearts and imaginations to the possibility of truly living our longing. That's the power of the poetry I love, the poetry of Rumi and Yeats and Neruda, of Mary Oliver and Annie Dillard and Susan Griffin and many others. Words themselves can become acts of beauty that awaken and strengthen our commitment to living our soul's desires.

But saying something we truly mean and being able to live it are two very different things. The older I get, the more I love words and trust actions. When I was young and I met a man, I wanted to know if he believed women were equal and entitled to the same choices as those afforded to men. Now, I am more interested in whether or not he'll cook some of the meals regularly and clean up after—including cleaning out the unidentifiable gunk that collects in the sink strainer—without making a big deal out of it. I am less interested in people's articulated spiritual beliefs or political philosophies and more interested in whether or not they are true to themselves even when it costs them something, whether or not they can be kind when it is easier to be indifferent, whether or not they can remember that to be human is to be flawed and spectacular and deeply compassionate.

If we cannot hear the music of our own sweet nature calling to us, if we cannot remember that the intention is to live who we really are, it's hard to know how to move, where to begin, how to dance. That's why it's not always a good idea to start shouting enthusiastically about what we are going to do, how we are going to live our soul's longing, no matter how strongly this longing is felt in the moment. Sometimes we need to just stand quietly together, hand in hand, until one of us hears the music and begins to dance.

### Meditation on Your Essential Nature

The purpose of this meditation is to gently expand your ability to extend to yourself the same compassionate understanding you extend to those you love.

Sit or lie down in a comfortable position, and bring your attention to your breathing, following the breath as it enters and leaves your body, letting your muscles release with each exhale. Do this for a dozen breaths, just following the rising and falling of your body with each breath.

Now, allow someone you know and love to come to mind. Let it be someone you know well, someone you have seen at their best and their worst, someone you love deeply. Allow yourself a moment to imagine this person in your mind's eye, feeling the love you have for them.

Then remember how this person behaves when they are not at their best, when they are deeply frightened and unable to be with the fear. Do they lash out at others or withdraw? Do they run from their pain or dive in and add to their suffering through self-recrimination? See them as they are in these moments, and feel how what they do does not change your love for them or color what you know of the best of them.

Now imagine how they would look in one of their worst moments to someone who does not know them—someone who might conclude that they are basically angry or needy or inconsiderate or cold—and tell this new person what it is you see and love in the one you know, who they are in their essential nature. Feel how you do not confuse their behavior with the essence of who they are. See them in your mind's eye becoming the person you are describing, the person you know them to be, shining in their essential nature—and let them go.

Now turn your attention to yourself, seeing yourself in your mind's eye as you did the other. Imagine yourself in one of your worst moments. What do you do when you are frightened and not able to simply be with the fear? Do you lash out or turn away from others? See yourself behaving badly, and imagine someone who does not know you also seeing you. What conclusions might they reach about who you are, seeing you like this and not knowing or loving you? Explain to the stranger who does not know you how this man, this woman they are seeing is behaving badly because they are deeply frightened or tired or lost in this moment. Tell them who this man or woman is in his or her essential nature—what he or she cares deeply about, how she or he loves, and how he or she wants to contribute to the world. As you describe your essential nature, see yourself at your best, in a moment when your actions are consistent with this nature. Ask yourself to gently consider, "What if this is who I really am? What if all I need to do is allow the unfolding of my essential nature? What if all I need to do is to become who I really am? What if this is enough?"

# TWO

# *Dancing with the Mystery*

~

*Show me how you follow your deepest desires,*
*spiraling down into the ache within the ache,*
*and I will show you how I reach inward and open outward*
*to feel the kiss of the Mystery, sweet lips on my own, every day.*

This is my secret that all other truth telling seeks to disguise: I have always felt the presence of that which is larger than myself.

This is my earliest clear memory: I am lying in bed, curled into a tight ball, listening with every cell in my body. I'm cold, but it's fear and not a lack of heat that chills me. I must be three or four years old, old enough to be sleeping in a bed without railings, young enough to have been put to bed while there is still enough light coming in through the window to see the color of the pale pink walls of my room. I can hear my parents arguing in the next room. I cannot make out their words, but I recognize the sounds of anger and tears. The periodic silences are worse than the words—a separation that threatens the wholeness of my world.

Although they do not seem young to me, my parents are only in their early twenties. Later, as an adult, I will appreciate how they weathered the stresses and strains of being married and having two small children at such a young age. Later, after I have been twice married and divorced, I will wonder how they stayed together, I will marvel that there weren't more arguments, and I will be grateful that there was no violence. Later, when I crawl into a dark corner beneath the desk in the apartment I share with my first husband, pulling my knees up under my chin and hoping to make myself so small he cannot pull me out and hit me again, I will think of my parents. And when my husband tries to convince me that all fledgling marriages are like ours, that behind closed doors all young couples are living with unhappiness and violence, I will almost believe him. Almost. What will save me is the memory of my parents who, even when they were young, argued without violence, laughed more than they cried, and played more than they fought.

But at three years of age, lying in the dark listening to the sound of their voices, I have no such perspective. I am simply frightened by the sound of their disagreement. I strain to hear their words, waiting for them to stop, willing them to turn toward each other. Gradually the anger in their voices is replaced with weariness and the silence is shared. Relieved but still worried, I cannot get to sleep. My body stays curled in a hard tight knot, and I can hear my own heart beating loudly. And so I pray to the God I've heard about in my Presbyterian Sunday school class. I ask him to keep us safe, to stop the fighting, to help me go to sleep. And as I pray, I begin to feel a presence with me in the room. It is a warm strength that surrounds my bed. My muscles relax into this presence that seems to hold me, and I imagine lying in a giant hand—the hand of God—there in my bed. And I fall asleep, held there by a great tenderness.

Calling on this presence becomes my way of coping with what I find hard in my young life. Anxiety is a normal part of every life, and sometimes I am simply overwhelmed with life and the world and all there is to learn. And every time I pray, every single time, I feel this presence of something that is greater than myself, there with me. Sometimes, if I am particularly upset about something that has happened during the day—a fight with my brother or doing something that had sparked my mother's formidable temper—I hear a voice as I drift off to sleep, a voice that seems to me to be a blending of many voices, male and female, a voice that calls me by name and fills me with a warmth that starts in my chest, there in the center of my small rib cage beneath my flannel nightgown, and spreads throughout my body. Seeming to come from both outside and inside me, the voice says, "We are always with you. We will always be with you." And I know it's true.

I don't tell anyone about my prayers or God's hand or the voice that comes to comfort me in the night. I'm not being particularly secretive. I assume that everyone has their way of knowing they are held by God when they can't get to sleep. I figure we don't talk about it for the same reason we don't talk about breathing—it's a given, just part of being alive.

As I get older my prayers become conversations. I ask questions, seek guidance. What should I do with my life? How can I make the world a better place? What's right, what's wrong? And I always hear answers. Oh, not definitive, "Do this!" kinds of answers. More often I hear within myself leading questions: What do you love to do? Who do you see that is suffering? How can you help? Sometimes there are short answers: "Breathe" or "let go" or "patience." And always there is this sense of a presence holding me, a sense of the voices that have promised they will always be there.

At fourteen I find out that not everyone is having this kind of experience. It comes as quite a shock. My best friend, Debbie, is the bearer of the bad news. "You just don't get it, do you?" she asks one day as we walk home together complaining about math homework, worrying about whether either of us will ever get a date, and talking about God. She states it flatly, defiantly, as if she just can't believe my stupidity. "No one else gets answers when they pray. They don't hear anything."

I don't get it. We live in a town of five thousand people that has at least eight churches attended regularly by almost everyone I know. Organized religion is a large part of the social fabric of the town, and even with my frustration with what seems to me to be often dull church services and dogmatic theology, I assume that beneath this the participants all have their version of my inner dialogue with something larger than themselves.

Debbie is emphatic. "The rest of us pray. We recite prayers in church, we say grace before meals, and we say prayers at bedtime. But most of us don't pray when we are alone, and even when we do, *we don't hear anything!*"

I am stunned and, for just a moment, afraid. What if one day I reach out and can't hear or feel anything? I can't imagine how anyone copes with the size of the world without this sense of the presence of something larger than themselves, and I am well aware that my anxieties were pretty minor compared with those who do not have a loving family or an adequate income. But the fear is momentary. All my life I have heard the voices reassure me that they will always be there, and I believe them.

What I hadn't counted on was the other half of this equation—my ability to reach out and listen—not always being as true. Nothing has fueled my efforts to cultivate a daily spiritual practice more than the memory of those times when I could not even remember to reach out to the presence that had held me, times when I was caught in a kind of bleak amnesia of the heart. It's not that I ever thought that this presence had abandoned me, but there were times during that first marriage in my early twenties when I just couldn't find the time or energy to turn my face back toward that steady loving strength. I was distracted by what felt like the sudden and terrifying necessity of deciding what I was going to do with my life and by the escalating violence in my marriage. I do remember on one occasion, as I literally flew through the air and hit the black and white tiles of the kitchen floor, thinking vaguely that there was something I needed to reach out for, something I needed to remember that would change everything. But I couldn't clear my head—or my heart—to remember what it was. Even the thought that there was anything to remember was gone as fast as it appeared, swallowed by the need to pull away from the darkness of the present moment—as if there is ever anyplace else to go.

It was my illness a few years later—ironically, largely a consequence of the violence in that marriage—that brought me back to a conscious cultivation of my connection with Spirit. Lying in bed ill can be a very lonely place. As I learned to consciously stay with the loneliness, to feel the unnameable longing, I remembered how I used to fall asleep held by the hand of God. And when I reached out the presence that had always been there, the voices that said they would never leave were right there with me once again. Perhaps sometimes we give up our loneliness too quickly, moving away from the ache before it can lead us back to the Beloved.

Once, when I told someone the story of my childhood sense of God's presence, they asked if I'd ever wondered if I was crazy, hearing voices in the night. I can honestly say that this never crossed my mind. Maybe that in itself isn't a good sign, but in all other things I appear to have been a normal if somewhat intense child. I did well at school, had friends and all the usual childhood ups and downs. It didn't seem strange to me that the God I heard so much about would communicate directly when called upon.

As an adult I came to realize how much this view offends some. A few years ago, a Protestant minister told me with great conviction that God had said everything he needed or wanted to say to those who had written the Bible. These were God's final words.

"But," I said, "given the state of the world—the suffering, the cruelty, the despair—it would appear that humans haven't heard what God was trying to say. Are you telling me that God, like an angry parent, is silently saying, 'If you didn't get it the first time, I'm not going to repeat myself'? That seems a little harsh. Wouldn't a loving God want to reveal his message to humans in as many different ways as possible to increase their chances of getting it?"

He was unmoved by my argument, adamantly insisting that no one today could directly experience God or God's message for us. This view seems to me now to be an almost inevitable consequence of seeing God as something or someone outside of and separate from ourselves. If who we are is not in some essential way an embodiment of the divine, surely we are unworthy or incapable of directly communicating with or experiencing this sacred presence.

Still, receiving guidance from something larger than ourselves can be a tricky business. It's easy to confuse the experience of our essential compassionate nature with a belief in our own divinity that borders on infallibility and denies our human inclination to hear what we want to hear when we send out a voice in prayer or meditation. The Native American elders with whom I have studied warn against our propensity to abdicate our responsibility in determining what we do with those things we have decided are signs or messages from the divine. I have met too many who justify their choices by the astrological reading of the day or how they interpreted the first thing that crossed their path after they asked a meditative question—a random phrase in a book, a call from a friend, a song on the radio. I would not eliminate these or any other seemingly unlike occurrences as environmental cues that help us probe more deeply the questions in our lives. But nothing in my childhood or adult experiences of this sacred presence within and around me has ever suggested that I am not fully responsible for all the choices I make. Easy answers were never given, only questions and suggestions that made me delve deeper into my own knowing.

To call this presence the Mystery is to be deliberately mindful that all the ideas we have about this presence are simply that—our ideas. I do not know what it is; I only know from my experience that it is, even as I use my imagination as a key to open the door to this experience.

Every day, sometimes when I am doing my meditation practice and sometimes when I am working at my computer or sitting in my car waiting for a traffic light to change or sharing a meal with friends, I turn my attention to my breath and visualize myself on some inner plane of the imagination turning my face toward that which is larger than myself—the Great Mystery. I only have to turn my face toward it. I become aware of the temperature of the air touching my cheek. I imagine the molecules of oxygen and hydrogen and carbon dioxide colliding in exuberant activity, caressing the skin of my face. And I become aware that these molecules are alive with a vibration, a presence that is there also in the cells of my skin and in the molecules of those cells and in the atoms and subatomic particles of those.

Slowly I turn my attention to an inner view of the landscape around and within me, and I become aware of this presence, like the hum of a great song constantly reverberating throughout and emanating from my body, the chair supporting me, the ground beneath me, and the people around me. And I know this presence as a whole that is larger than the sum of the parts and yet inseparable from the parts—including me—which are in a state of constant change. And I experience this presence, this bloodred thread of being that runs through the dark tapestry of daily life, as that which gives me the ability to truly know each other as another myself—as compassion.

When I open myself fully to the awareness of this presence, my shoulders drop a little and my belly softens and releases the accumulated deposits of small daily worries that build up in my insides like mineral deposits from hard-water springs. If I stay with my awareness of this presence, I know it as the heat at the center of life, as the innate orgiastic joy that shouts "Live!" even as it spends itself fully. I know it as the essence, the very stuff of which I, and everything that exists, am made, and I remember that this—this Mystery that is sacred—is who and what we are.

Although my experience of this presence has remained essentially the same throughout the years, my ideas and ways of describing it have changed. Exposure to the beliefs of other religions and my own development as a woman challenged the idea of God as a transcendent divine male person. But the presence around and within me remained the same when I turned my attention to it. In my late twenties and early thirties I began having vivid dreams of a council of old women I called the Grandmothers. They directed me to a shaman, a Native American medicine man living in the United States, who became my teacher. My love of the wilderness drew me to his earth-based teachings and practices, which were rooted in the land I love. Given this and my interest in the empowerment of the feminine in my own life and in the world, it is perhaps not surprising that the presence and the voices of these Grandmothers in the dream became a part of, a particular expression of, that greater presence that had always been with me.

Because I experience this Mystery as something constant and all-pervading, my words, which are necessarily limited, cannot capture its nature even if I could on some level know what it is. Describing my experience of the Sacred as the kiss of the Mystery is a metaphor, an approximation of the experience I am trying to share. Describing it instead as an experience of the imagined vibrations of molecules and subatomic particles around and within me is no less a metaphor. My choice of metaphor may color your understanding of what I am trying to convey, may even change my experience of it, but it does not change the reality of that presence. When we are frightened or suffering, the sense of this presence as someone may offer more comfort to our humanness than a more abstract idea of something. Some find comfort and guidance by naming and experiencing this presence as God, Allah, Christ, the Great Mother, Buddha consciousness. Humans have literally thousands of names and images for their experience of the Sacred.

*This is all I really know: there is a presence that is larger than myself that has been with me all my life.* I experience this presence as loving, and in some essential way it is what I am.

Many of the people I know experience this presence in their lives in ways they would never label spiritual—by the way they see and cherish all that is green and alive on the planet, through their participation in the ecstatic struggle of creativity, by giving themselves to a greater beauty in shape or color or sound or word. Some longing within us is met when we participate in the beauty of creation by really paying attention. It connects us to the presence of that which is unnameable. Beneath all our longings, the ache within the ache is a soul-deep desire to live within an awareness of this presence that is larger than ourselves, every moment.

But our prayers are the prayers of human beings and are rarely so grand. When we are unemployed and worried about providing for our children, our sincerest prayer may be a plea for money or a job. When we drop beneath these immediate and legitimate concerns, we find a longing to know that we belong to a community, that we are not isolated and on our own, prey to the real or imagined vagaries of the marketplace or uncertainties of the world. And beneath this real desire for support and community is a longing for contact with that which supports and connects us all—the Great Mystery.

I am not denigrating our very human needs as less than our longing for the Sacred. One of the students I have worked with for many years, a woman in her early fifties, lost her mother and her brother when she was fifteen. They were killed in a car accident. Often when she does ceremony, the grief over this loss and the longing for her mother are touched again, opening the wound that never heals within her. At one retreat I sat with her as she sobbed uncontrollably. When she could speak she said to me, "Sometimes I wonder if I confuse my longing for my mother with my longing for Spirit."

And I said, "Same longing."

We see God in the face of the child or mate or parent we cherish; we feel held by the Mystery when a lover or friend—or sometimes more acutely when a caring stranger—extends a hand and opens their heart to us. And yet, to meet the deeper need we feel, we must not burden these relationships, which are of necessity impermanent and ever changing, with the weight of unmet desires for what is constant and

ever-present. This most often happens in romantic relationships, perhaps because the fire of sexual intimacy when we are in love is so similar to—is an exquisite embodiment of—the ecstasy of feeling those
sweet lips of the Mystery on our own.

Jai Uttal, a gifted musician and singer, leads three hundred people in Hindu chants to the goddess Sita and the god Ram at a retreat
in upstate New York. I am not Hindu, but I sing these beautiful
unfamiliar names of the presence I know to the rhythm of the drum
and harmonium. What I love about these chants is that they are declarations of devotion to the divine. Once in a while my own prayers
can sound just a little too much like a grocery list of need. We sing
for over an hour, and I am filled with awareness of the Beloved
around me and within me. Beneath the chant a voice sings, "You are
mine."

Later, alone in my cabin, I lie in the dark and remember my name.

*Oriah* is a name that was given to me when I was thirty years old by
the Grandmothers in the dream. I had been ill with chronic fatigue
immune deficiency syndrome for several years, and when I awoke
from the dream I felt that taking this new name was part of the healing I so desperately sought. But it frightened me. It all just seemed
too weird, too flaky. I was afraid of what others would think. Despite
my fear, a week later I changed my name. When I asked the women
in my dreams what the name meant, they simply shook their heads
and said, "Not time."

Over the next ten years, unexpectedly and irregularly, the
Grandmothers in the dream would tell me something about the
meaning of my name. The last time, about six years ago, one of them
said, "Your name means She Who Belongs to God." I knew she could

have used the word *Mystery* or *Beloved* with equal conviction, and I wondered if the term *God* was a deliberate reminder of my childhood experiences.

As I lie in bed after the Hindu chanting I think again about the meaning of my name—of how it is true for all of us. We belong to God—to the sacred life force. I repeat my name to myself, whispering into the darkness, "Oriah, She Who Belongs to God . . . She Who Belongs to the Beloved . . . She Who Belongs to the Great Mystery . . . " And I begin to imagine what it might be like to live every day, to direct my actions, choose my words, and see the world as one who remembers that she belongs to, is an embodiment of, and is connected to that which is sacred and larger than herself. How would she treat her own body and heart? How would she treat the other embodiments of the Sacred—other people, the trees and animals, the earth? How would you plan your day if you really knew you *belonged* to God, if you believed you were an embodiment of the sacred Mystery, surrounded and held by the Beloved?

I do not seek perfection. I simply seek to remember who and what I am every day. I seek the people and places and practices that support the expanding of this awareness in my day, in my life, in my choices. Our lives are the story of how we remember. It is the dance that was woven into the fabric of our being from the beginning. The presence of the Great Mystery is always with us. I only have to turn my face toward it, and it is there—as a voice beneath the sound of the pale gray waves crashing on the shore, as a touch of the unseen on the back of my neck that makes me pause and turn as I cut carrots on my kitchen counter, as a kiss that lingers as I come up out of dreams in the mist of dark mornings.

## Meditation for Awareness

Sometimes opening our awareness to the sacred life force that is both within and around us is as simple as turning our attention to it as we would turn our face toward someone when we enter a room.

So, try this wherever you are at the moment. Without preparation or expectation, simply turn your attention to the skin of your own face. Be aware of the temperature of the air where it touches your cheek, your forehead, your lips and eyes. Imagine the air currents moving around your face, touching your skin, being changed, rerouted by any movement you make. Slowly turn your face, and be aware of the change in sensation there, where the air touches your skin.

Now imagine the molecules that make up that air where it touches your skin—the molecules of oxygen and hydrogen and carbon dioxide colliding with one another and bouncing against your skin. Imagine the atoms that make up those molecules, and see them vibrating with the movement of subatomic particles—spinning electrons and shimmering quirks and quarks. Be aware of this vibration as a consistent life force energy in all the different molecules of the air touching your face, surrounding you.

Now, keeping one part of your attention on the air around you, imagine this same kind of vibration in the cells of the skin the air is touching. Imagine the molecules of those cells vibrating at the level of their atoms and subatomic particles. Expand the awareness of this life force energy throughout your body—down your neck, through the muscles of your torso, and down your arms and legs. Imagine this same vibration in the organs within your body—in the cells and the molecules and the atoms of your lungs and stomach and heart. Feel your whole body as a manifestation of this same life force that vibrates in the molecules of the air around you.

Now, keeping one part of your attention on the vibration in your body and in the air around you, be aware of any objects around you—the ground beneath you, the chair you are sitting on, other people in the vicinity. Slowly, taking them in one at a time while maintaining the sense of the presence of the life force moving in all the cells of your body, become aware of the same source of vibration moving throughout the molecules of that which is around you. Be aware of the large—the trees, the wall, the ground beneath you—and the small—the single blade of grass, grains of sand and dirt, dust motes in the air. Be aware of the innate vibration of the microcosms within each of these, of how the same force sends their electrons spinning through inner space. Feel how the force behind the wind that tosses the branches of a tree is the same as that which makes the air moving in and out of your lungs eddy and flow. Imagine the flow of life-giving liquids moving up and down the trunk of a tree, and feel how this movement comes from the same source as that which moves the blood throughout your body.

Expand your awareness even further, letting your attention touch it all—the life force that moves and creates and sustains all that is within and around you. Feel how the whole is greater than the sum of the parts, embodied within you and yet larger than yourself. Be aware of how this presence is constant whether or not you turn your attention to it. Be aware of how it holds you faithfully.

# THREE

# Out of Step

*Don't tell me you want to hold the whole world in your heart.*
*Show me how you turn away from making another wrong without*
*abandoning yourself when you are hurt and afraid of being unloved.*

Making another wrong is a choice to put that person out of your heart. It's the kind of judgment that says to the self or the other, "You're a jerk, a piece of shit! There is something seriously and fundamentally wrong with you!"

There are ways to communicate these things, to make aspects of ourselves or the other wrong without ever uttering such crude words. Those of us who have done years of therapy and self-growth seminars know how to cloak the judgments that wound and separate with cleverly crafted "I" statements, avoiding accusatory "you" statements or blatantly vicious self-deprecation. But the judgment is still there in the tone of the voice, like a razor-sharp sword that sweeps low, cutting the other off at the knees while calmly looking her in the eyes. It is there in the way we hold our bodies, in the slight tilt of the head, in the narrowing of our eyes when we regard the other or look in the mirror. It is there in the way we spend ourselves on too much work that doesn't matter, in relationships where we are not cared for or seen. It says the same thing to the other or to the self: *you are not enough.*

In the morning I meditate and soften my breath and reach out to hold those who are suffering, to hold the frightened aspects of myself and the world in my heart. And then I head out into my day, praying I will remember the compassion I am, hoping I will be able to keep my heart open. Some days are better than others.

I am having breakfast at a retreat. I introduce myself to two men already sitting at a table, and we begin to share a little about ourselves over scrambled eggs and hot tea. A tall attractive man with a Texas drawl joins us and introduces himself as Sam. When I tell him my name his eyes light up. "Oriah? Did you write 'The Invitation'?" Through the ever-expanding network of e-mail contacts someone had sent him a copy of a prose poem I had written. "It's great to meet you," he says enthusiastically, pulling a camera from beneath his coat. "I really want to capture this moment."

I wince at the sight of the camera and hold up my hand. "Sorry, Sam. I really dislike having my picture taken at the very best of times, and believe me, breakfast is not the best of times." I am smiling pleasantly, but I am clear and firm. "Why don't you sit down and join us for breakfast." He sits down next to me, camera still in hand.

"Ah, come on. There are times when you just have to capture the moment on film." He raises the camera to his eye and begins to adjust the focus.

"No. Really, I don't enjoy having my picture taken. I'm serious— I really don't want my picture taken."

He continues to adjust the focus, leaning back and forth in the chair to get different angles. "This is important. You just have to do this!" His tone is insistent and increasingly aggressive. The men on the other side of the table shift uncomfortably in their seats as I look at them and shake my head, bewildered. I just do not know how to get through to him.

He persists. For five minutes he insists over and over that he must take my picture. I feel my face growing tense under the strain of trying to smile, trying to keep my tone firm but neutral as I say no again and again. Ignoring my protests, he clicks the shutter and takes a picture, and I feel something inside me give up. All other conversation at the table has become impossible. Finally, wanting simply for the whole thing to be over, I sit still and he takes ten to fifteen shots. I know they will be awful. I have closed some part of myself and sit and simply endure. The photos will reflect this.

I leave the table angry and upset. Later in the day I run into a friend and tell him about what happened. He is sympathetic, and we agree that the man was invasive. I feel a little better.

That night as I lie in bed I replay the whole incident in my mind. Internally I rail on about what a jerk this guy was, imagining all kinds of things I could have or should have said or done. I should have grabbed his camera after he started shooting and flipped it open, ruining the film. I should have stood up and in a loud voice announced to the whole dining room, "What part of *no* don't you understand?"

And then I stop. All day I have been meditating on loving-kindness. It's relatively easy and appealing to think of holding the sick or the poor or the suffering parts of the world or me in my heart. But what about this guy Sam? I feel no compassion for him. My heart feels hard when I think of him pushing me. He did not respect my boundaries. But let's face it, it was a photo, not a physical attack. I had every right to insist that I did not want my picture taken, but was there a way to communicate this to him without making him The Jerk, something less than another human being, another myself? I struggle with this. How do you tell someone compassionately to fuck off? I don't want to see Sam as another myself. I feel certain I would never insist on taking pictures of someone without their permission.

I sit up in bed and flip the light on, disturbed by the fact that I cannot see any way to truly feel I am holding this man in my heart. Saying it or thinking it is not enough. What good are all the meditations on compassion if I cannot find a way to keep my heart open to someone who simply annoys the hell out of me? If I can't do this, how can I hope to be compassionate to those who do me or others real harm?

I find a comfortable sitting position, close my eyes, and focus on my breath. I am determined to sit and mediate until I find some connection to Sam. I am not looking for a warm fuzzy feeling. I am searching for an awareness of Sam as another myself, as a fellow human being I can consciously hold in my heart.

It takes a long time, and I begin to despair. The room is getting cold, and I really just want to go to sleep. When I think of the morning's incident all I feel is anger and dislike. I feel nothing I can identify with in Sam's behavior. I begin to pray. "Sacred Ones, help me find some way not to put this man out of my heart." I wait. I breathe. I repeat my prayer. A question comes: Why did Sam ignore the clear boundaries I set? Why didn't he care that his actions were violating these boundaries? I know the answer immediately: because he wanted what he wanted—a decent picture and a personal connection with me in that moment—very badly. Ironically, by insisting, he destroyed any chance of getting either.

Suddenly I think of my sons when they were small, how they could become fixated on something they wanted and beg and wheedle and press long after *no* had been repeated many times, making me angry and destroying any chance of getting what they wanted then or later. I remember Nathan's first and only temper tantrum at the age of three, his young body exploding with the rage of unmet demands. Did I put either of them out of my heart because they were irritating and demanding? No. Did I acquiesce to their demands? No. There was usually a good reason why I had said no in the first place, and those reasons were not changed by their insistence.

Remembering my sons opens the narrowest crack of possibility that I am capable of holding someone in my heart even when they are demanding something of me that I am unable or unwilling to give. Suddenly I see Sam as another of my sons, out of control with wanting things his own way in this moment and consequently acting in a way that guarantees he will not get what he wants. And my heart begins to soften to his humanness, to the suffering he causes himself.

And I think of the times I have wanted things to be a certain way— my way. How, near the end of my second marriage, I wanted— ached—to have my husband talk to me, hold me, spend time with me at the end of the day when he was too weary and discouraged to want to do anything but withdraw and be alone. How I would pursue him, overtly and covertly, asking, pressing, insisting, accusing, all the while knowing that my actions were creating more distance between us and yet, in my desperation, unable to stop.

The situations are different, but the motivation that drives each of us to override the wishes of others—wanting our way—remains the same. Suddenly I could see Sam as simply a fellow human being in a bad moment, and I could hold in my heart the part of him that I had seen, the desperately grasping child afraid he will not get what he wants, just as I can hold my sons and myself in my heart when we insist on having things our way.

Softening to Sam, I could risk seeing my own behavior of the morning much more clearly. No longer needing to make him The Jerk, I no longer needed to make myself The Virtuous Victim. Why hadn't I simply gotten up and moved to another table? Because I was at least a little flattered by the attention of an attractive man. The others at the table had never heard of my poem, and his enthusiastic response let everyone know they were sitting with a Writer. Then later, in soliciting my friend's agreement with my rendition of the event, I was able to feel a sense of my rightness in proportion to how wrong Sam was.

I groan, laugh out loud, and, clicking the light off, slide down under the covers. My own self-importance did as much to create the situation as Sam's insistence on having things his way. I shake my head at our humanness.

As compassionate beings, we have the ability to hold all aspects of ourselves and the world in our hearts, including those aspects that are annoying, dangerous, malicious, and just downright unlikable. But we have to be willing to do the work of finding out *how* to do this, honestly observing our own internal and external actions and reactions and learning from each instance how to expand our ability to live the compassion we are.

Think of all the places where you separate yourself from others, distinguishing between "us" and "them." The minute we do this we are building our sense of self, not on what we truly are, but on trying to feel better than others because we fear we are not enough. I watch myself do this all the time. And if I watch with honesty and compassion, I find a way to make being right an unnecessary prerequisite for being happy.

I have been an outspoken critic of some New Age spirituality. I don't like sloppy thinking, a refusal to ask questions, or an easy acceptance of things we cannot know to be true because we find them comforting or far more entertaining than our everyday lives, and I have seen too much of all of this in some New Age philosophies and groups. I think it's dangerous.

Of course there is some truth in all of these judgments, and I will continue to raise questions about the claims made by all spiritual paths because I am interested in learning the truth as far as we can know it. But there are ways to raise questions that open inquiry—that make it "our" inquiry—and other ways to pose questions that close down communication. And there are ways intended to distinguish between "us" and "them," ways that aim to make me feel right—more authentic, grounded, and intelligent—by making the other wrong.

A few months ago I attended a day-long talk given by a well-known New Age speaker. The bookseller at the event had asked me to come and help out at the book table after the presentation. Entertaining and personable, the speaker had drawn a crowd of several hundred and gave a lecture introducing the ideas and practices of many different traditional spiritual teachers mixed with her own New Age philosophy. The audience was enthralled, and I was doing my best to keep an open mind. I knew that what this woman offered was basically an introduction, an open door. I did not agree with many of her beliefs, and her absolute certainty that each of us creates and controls every aspect of our lives made me uneasy. More important, her lavishly guaranteed outcomes for anyone willing to follow the nine steps of her program or do the daily affirmations she offered made me more than a little uncomfortable. Guaranteed outcomes and delineated steps may be warranted and useful for baking cookies and assembling bookshelves, but I find them less useful and potentially misleading when we are talking about finding meaning and creating happiness in our own lives and in the world.

I kept looking around at the participants, many of whom were nodding with what I was pretty sure was uncritical and unexamined enthusiasm. I felt my desire and inclination to separate myself from them. Were they buying this? Why would they even want to? Surely they knew that there were no easy answers, no simple steps that would cure all that was unhappy in their lives. Maybe *they* were just lazy. Even as I made the separation I was aware of it, reaching to find a way not to close my heart to those around me, not to write *them* off in my mind as less than those of *us* who know that spiritual development can be hard, that there are no easy answers.

After the event I worked at the book table, chatting with people as they were leaving. One woman approached as I packed up my things and asked me about one of the meditation techniques the speaker had advocated. It was a relatively simple morning meditation designed to still the mind and focus on the breath, and the speaker had guaranteed that using it regularly would deliver the power to manifest whatever you wanted in your life.

A small thin woman in an oversized parka, she introduced herself as Isabel. "Can I do this meditation on my own?" she asked.

"Yes," I said. "I am sure you can, although many people find it easier to establish a meditation practice with the help of a group. It's just hard to keep up the discipline on your own."

"But what will it give me? What will I get if I do this every day?" Her tone took on a whining quality, and I felt my irritation rise as she continued. "How fast will it work? Will I feel a difference after a week? How will I know if it's working?"

This was exactly the kind of thing I detested—the quest for the quick fix, the desire for guaranteed outcomes, the simple answer. Do this and you will get that. These were, I thought, exactly the expectations a presentation like the one I had just seen raised. And where was the woman who had raised them? Gone, leaving me to answer questions for which there are no short, simple answers. My sons were waiting for me, and I wanted to go home.

I took a deep breath, looked directly at Isabel, and set my knapsack down on the floor. I tried to slow down my words, thinking that maybe if I spoke slower I would feel more patient. "Well," I said, "meditation is more a process than a goal-oriented activity. It can help you become more aware of what is going on within and around you, and this can help reduce stress. There is no way to know how quickly this will happen. I have been meditating for years, and some days my mind is all over the place, and other days I have a real sense of rest and peace. My best advice is to try it and just be patient with yourself." I picked up my bag and started to button my coat. I really did have to leave, and I wanted to get out while I was feeling virtuous for not snapping her head off.

But as I started to move away Isabel suddenly reached out and grabbed my arm with surprising strength. "But, what I want to know," she said, her voice rising in a crescendo that bordered on real panic, "is will it help me find God? If I meditate, will I have an experience of something or someone out there listening, something really with me?"

A wave of desperation swept out from her through me, and I was surprised to find my eyes filling with tears. This woman wasn't looking for an easy answer or a guaranteed formula because she was lazy. She didn't want a simple plan because she was unable or unwilling to think critically about what would work. She wanted something she knew would work and work quickly because she was hanging on by her fingernails. She wanted something that would work in a week because she was afraid that she simply wasn't going to make it through months or years. She wanted to know—to experience—that there really was something greater than herself, and she was afraid, terrified that if she didn't have an experience of this soon she was not going to able to continue. I recognized another myself: the self that is at times at the edge of her endurance, not at all sure that continuing is possible; the self that is in so much pain that taking the next breath and the next feels like all the challenge she can meet.

I put my hand gently over Isabel's where it gripped my arm. "It's okay, Isabel, we all feel desperate at times," I said. "Nobody does it by themselves. We all need help." Her hand relaxed beneath mine, and she started to cry. We talked for a while longer, and I gave her the name of a few meditation teachers who run small groups in the city, encouraging her to find a community where she could feel supported. When I left, I did not leave one of *them*. I said good-bye to one of *us*, a human being doing the best she can, searching for the home for which all our hearts long.

There is no them. There's only us. When we separate ourselves from those aspects of humanity we do not like, we do so primarily out of fear that those aspects live in us. And the truth is, they do.

On the way home from this event I began to think about the rest of the audience. Some of them, no doubt, were not desperately searching like Isabel, were probably wanting easy answers and entertainment because they did not want to do the work of cultivating the spiritual aspect of their lives. No longer needing to separate myself from *them*, I began to think about the places where I want an easy answer and a guaranteed outcome because I don't want to do the work. Physical exercise immediately came to mind as I thought of all the money I have spent on health club memberships, exercise equipment, and a variety of workout videos, only to find that spending the money won't get you in shape; you actually have to exercise. Was I really too stupid to know this? Of course not. I simply didn't want to do the work.

Recognizing that I can be lazy about physical exercise just like some others may be lazy about spiritual practice does not let any of us off the hook. Understanding Sam's behavior and remembering that I too am capable of trampling others' boundaries when I am fixated on having things my way does not mean that either Sam or I is excused when we do this. It just means it is *our* human problem and not just *his,* even though he may be the one acting it out in this moment. Having compassion does not mean indiscriminately accepting or going along with others' actions regardless of the consequences to us or the world. It is about being able to say no where we need to without putting the other out of our hearts, without making the other less of a fellow human being. There is a difference between discerning and sometimes even opposing harmful behavior and making the other wrong—less than we are, less a part of that presence that is greater than all of us—in our own minds and hearts.

Sam and Isabel were both strangers, people I did not know. While our brief interactions challenged my ability to be with them compassionately, I did not have a relationship with either of them that made me vulnerable to being deeply hurt by their actions. Keeping our hearts open to the other who has hurt us is harder. The deeper the love, the more profound the hurt and the harder it is to turn away from making the other wrong. And there are covert ways to cast another out of our hearts: we tell our friends, especially the mutual acquaintances, how we have been wronged, denying or ignoring any responsibility for our part in the story; we take pleasure in hearing of small failures suffered by the other.

I am not suggesting that we should pretend to be more magnanimous than we are. A friend whose partner recently left her told me a week after the breakup, "I really do wish him well."

"Bullshit," I said. "Too soon. You don't wish him well. Right now you hope he's miserable and lonely and sitting at home feeling destroyed because he has just realized that he's lost the best woman he could ever hope to have in his life."

She laughed. "Well, yes, I guess that's true. But I want to wish him well—someday."

"And you probably will," I replied, laughing with her. "But for now, stay with how hurt and angry you are. Sit with these feelings and how this happened—what your part was, what his part was—and how you have both hurt each other and at times yourselves."

We cannot start from any place other than where we are. This is the work of compassion—finding a way not to put my self or the other out of my heart, letting go of the need to be right, resisting the urge to shame the other when I am hurt without denying my own pain.

Recently I failed to do this with my friend Sharon. The particulars are unimportant. I knew I had to remove myself from the relationship, but I was unaware of how hurt I was still feeling over something she had done. Being unconscious about how we are feeling, while never an excuse for anyone over forty, can be dangerous. It wasn't so much what I said; in fact, my words flawlessly addressed the behavior that necessitated my departure. But the tone of one sentence as it flew from my mouth, aimed to wound her spirit, said that there was something essentially wrong with her, that she was not enough.

I'll tell you something you should probably know: the more consistently conscious I am of the compassion that is my essential nature, the more I ache when my own pain makes me forget this nature and lash out and make another wrong as I did with Sharon. This is what it means to be heartsick: to act contrary to our nature. And there is no way to take it back, no way to reassure the other that you have not put them out of your heart—because you did, if only for a moment. And then you are left, as I am now, struggling not to put out of my heart that aspect of myself that could so effectively hurt someone I love.

The Catholic priest Henri Nouwen wrote,

Forgiveness is the name of love practiced among people who love poorly. The hard truth is that all of us love poorly. We need to forgive and be forgiven every day, every hour—unceasingly. That is the great work of love among the fellowship of the weak that is the human family.

In my humanness I forget that who I am is enough, especially when I am hurt or afraid of being unloved. Immersed in the pain and fear that are part of this forgetting, I sometimes hurt another. Yet even this failure, for which I must take responsibility, calls me not to change but to be who I am, to hold myself within my innately compassionate heart. And I learn about the expansiveness of who we are, an expansiveness that makes us capable of compassion where we thought it was impossible.

It was the man who raped me when I was twenty-two who gave me the opportunity to learn this. I will tell you the truth. I do not even try by my own will to hold this man in my heart. When I think of him—and I do even now, years later, when I hear the story of another woman who has been raped—I simply see, in meditation, this man and me held by the heart of that which is larger than and yet a part of myself. I breathe, and I let the larger heart that has always held me, that is embodied in my essence, hold my pain and my anger. And when I do this, I catch a glimpse of the suffering—the anguish—there must be inside the human being who has raped another. Knowing this, I cannot help but remember that this man was once, like my own sons, some woman's child with hopes and fears. And it is not as impossible as I once thought it would be to pray and cry, not just for me, but also for him.

While there are important differences of degree in the injury we do one another, I am not so sure there are differences in kind. This is what makes cultivating my ability to hold myself and others in my heart when we commit relatively small hurts against ourselves and each other so important. What hope do I have of not closing my heart to the man who raped me or to myself when I hurt someone I love if I cannot resist the impulse to make wrong the stranger who has annoyed me with his camera and his human need?

Alexander Solzhenitsyn, after suffering the horrors of a Siberian prison camp, wrote:

If only it were all so simple! If only there were evil people somewhere insidiously committing evil deeds, and it were necessary only to separate them from the rest of us and destroy them. But the line dividing good and evil cuts through the heart of every human being. And who is willing to destroy a piece of his own heart?

## *Meditation to Cultivate Compassion*

It's important when doing this meditation to begin with something small—some inadvertent slight that annoyed you or a passing irritation that made you angry but did not cause you deep pain. Eventually, you may want to do this meditation for more serious injuries to others or the self, but it's a good idea to begin with things that are relatively minor.

Sit comfortably and focus on your breath. Take three large breaths in through the nose, and exhale through the mouth, letting your shoulders drop and letting any stress or tension leave your body. Spend a couple of minutes following your breath.

Now, think back over the last few days of your life. Let your mind find a time when someone annoyed or irritated you, an incident in which your internal response was to dismiss the other as a jerk. It may have been a total stranger—someone who cut you off in traffic or took your parking space at work or gave you poor service in a restaurant or store. Life is full of opportunities to be annoyed with one another. It may be someone you know—a partner who forgot to take the garbage out, a child who ate the dessert for tomorrow night's dinner party, a friend who was late and kept you waiting. Stay with something small.

Focus on this incident and the flash of anger or annoyance you felt. Be aware of what it feels like to put another out of your heart, if only for a moment. Let your self replay the incident and expand the internal railing against the other's inconsiderateness.

Now decide: Do you want to find a way to have compassion for this other person in the situation that annoyed you? Are you willing to see another you in their behavior?

If you are, begin to see the situation from that person's perspective. You may have little or no information about why they behaved as they did. Use your imagination. Consider the essence of what they did—was it careless, reckless, inconsiderate of others? Consider why you sometimes—possibly under very different circumstances—behave recklessly, carelessly, or in a manner that does not consider others. Perhaps it is when you are tired or pressured or angry or frightened. Work with the possibilities until you can see another you in the behavior of this person who annoyed and irritated you. When you can do this, imagine holding yourself and this other in your heart when you are tired or frightened or angry. Remember you do not need to condone the behavior, but simply hold in your heart this other and yourself when either of you is struggling with this particular challenge of being human.

# FOUR

# The Dancer

*Tell me a story of who you are,*
*and see who I am in the stories I am living.*
*And together we will remember that each of us always has a choice.*

I trust stories. The stories we choose to tell about ourselves let the world know who we are because who we are is not in what we do but in how we live. And this is what shapes the world.

It's October 1963, and I am nine years old. My family has just moved to a new town four hundred miles north of where we were living, and it is my first day at the new school. My teacher, Mrs. Lawson, a maternal gray-haired woman with a soft voice, takes me to the indoor play area. The children have been allowed into the large room—boys on one side, girls on the other—because the day is rainy and cold. The whole area is a din of high-pitched voices bouncing off concrete walls, a smelly soup of small sweaty bodies and wet wool. I follow Mrs. Lawson's broad backside as it cuts a swath through the sea of children until she comes to two girls. "Jill and Patsy, this is the new girl. I want you to look after her and show her where to go."

I turn to the girls, ready to smile. Jill has a round flushed face like a red full moon. She keeps shifting her gaze between Patsy and me, watching us closely. Clearly Patsy is the one in charge. Patsy is a petite cool blond with pale blue eyes. She does not smile as she looks me up and down. Their indifference borders on hostility, and my stomach turns over. I am unprepared for this. At my old school I had been at the top of the class, the belle of the ball upon occasion, at least on the playground. Oh, I'd had my contests, and I'd not always won: Cindy Morris, a small and wiry girl, once beat me up for no apparent reason and then sat astride me and crowed; Betty Ann Brown had tried to snub me, but we both knew that I was smarter and there were only so many friends she could buy with all that allowance her parents gave her; and Joey Peterson—what we called in those days a little roughneck—sometimes chased us girls, but in all fairness we did taunt him and then get him into trouble by telling on him when his chasing scared us.

But these trials and tribulations had had a kind of law-of-the-jungle-lord-of-the-flies sort of fairness about them. This, this assessment by Mademoiselles Patsy and Jill, was something else. I was clearly not passing muster, but I didn't know the criteria by which I was being judged.

As I stood there watching the looks-like-a-loser glances pass between Patsy and Jill, suddenly a dark-eyed gypsy appeared at my side. She smiled at me with a lopsided grin, two teeth missing, and said, "That's okay, Mrs. Lawson, I'll show her where to go," and then introduced herself as Ruth. She was my savior, my angel. Ruth had long dark hair that was an uncombed mass of curls and tangles, and she greeted me as if she were genuinely happy I was there, as if she had been waiting for me. I was overwhelmed with gratitude not to be given to the tender attentions of Jill and Patsy.

Ruth took me to the classroom, showed me where to hang my coat and put my lunch box, and then led me to a desk at the back of the room next to her own. As I sat down I was aware of the other kids eyeing me up and down, but I figured that was natural. A new kid in class always piques curiosity. But there was something else, an eyebrow shooting up here and there as faces took in Ruth and me together.

I was an innocent. Really. I don't know how I had gotten this far—fourth grade—without an awareness of the social class system, but I was oblivious. Perhaps it was because up to this point we had lived in a small city where the school I attended was filled with kids from a pretty homogeneous working-class neighborhood. Perhaps it was because my father's skilled job and secure employment put us near the top of that working-class heap. I don't know. But in a small town it was different. All the families sent their kids to the same school—rich and poor, white collar and blue, welfare recipient and business owner. And then there was the distinction I would learn about in time, between interlopers like us from the south and true northerners, those who were at least third generation.

Maybe it was just my time—that time when we all learn the hard truth about how shitty our species can be to each other, how quickly and rigidly people of all ages like to establish a clear pecking order. The first indication of stratification came at lunch. There were those who smugly ordered and paid for their milk—chocolate or white—in ten-cent pints. And then there were those who, with an almost imperceptible cringing, received their milk free, white only, because they had been identified as those in need—poor. And then there were my brother and me. We frugally brought our milk—white only—in thermoses. This marked us as the outsiders we were and meant we had to carry a stale-smelling lunch box to and from school every day no matter how many thermos liners we broke.

Ruth took a bus to school and got her milk for free. And Ruth smelled. She was bright and funny and one of the bravest girls I ever knew, but she smelled. I hadn't noticed it that first morning, what with all the mingling of the masses in the play space, but when we ate lunch together I caught a whiff. It's the scent my son Nathan calls the smell of poverty, the smell that makes him refuse to shop at Goodwill for used clothes even though I assure him we can wash or dry-clean the smell right out of any designer buys we find. It's the smell of unwashed bodies and clothes worn too often without airing or cleaning.

My grandmother used to say, "There's no excuse for being dirty no matter how poor you are. Soap is cheap." But keeping clean is as much about hope as it is about hygiene. My grandmother had been poor during the Depression, surrounded by thousands of others who were struggling but still hoping and dreaming. What I could smell on Ruth, what Nathan smells at Goodwill, is the hopelessness of being poor when you are surrounded by others with plenty.

I don't know how long it took me to figure it out—no more than a week, I'm sure—but I knew that if I wanted to have any place with the rest of the girls in my class I was going to have to ditch Ruth. She was an outcast, at the bottom of the social ladder because she was poor, because her family lived in a shack on the edge of town, because her mother and father were alcoholics living on welfare and it was rumored that her older sister was pregnant with her own father's child.

I didn't really have any feelings about any of these things. Some of them I didn't even understand. My concerns were all selfish. I didn't want to be ostracized because some lonely girl—even one I liked—

had glommed on to me, even if that glomming had felt like being rescued at the time.

There was a gully out behind the school where the boys and girls used to play and fight, throwing each other down with screams and threats and more screams. I was a bit of a chickenshit, so I tried to stay out of the way, but one day this boy Snyder—a boy I swear to you looked sixteen in grade six and had enormous gorillalike nostrils—gets me and starts twirling me around by the scarf tied at my neck, preparing to slingshot me into the ice-filled gully, when Ruth fearlessly flings herself at the back of his knees and tackles him. He lets go of my scarf, and the two of them tumble to the bottom of the gully, where Ruth, covered in snow, her mittenless hands raw from the cold, starts waving to me and hollering, "We got him! We got him!" Her inclusion of me in this victory is beyond generosity—it's an attempt to forge a bond in the face of the enemy—and the real enemy is not Snyder, and she knows it.

Later, maybe the same day—I hope it was several days later, but I really can't remember—I have just climbed up out of the gully and see Ruth coming up behind me. The slope is slippery, so I wait for her to reach a place where she can take my hand and be pulled to level ground. And as I wait I suddenly hear a couple of other girls moving toward the school—it may even have been Jill and Patsy—calling, "Come on. Let's go." To my surprise, they are calling and motioning to me to join them. I hesitate and look down at Ruth. She has seen them also.

There are moments when it doesn't matter if you are nine or nineteen or ninety. You know you are responsible for what you are about to do, you know what is right, and you know you are going to do what is wrong because you are afraid to take the consequences of doing what is right. I knew if I waited and helped Ruth I would be inextricably linked to her at the bottom of the social ladder, and there would be no more invitations to "come on" from further up that ladder.

I looked at her, she looked at me, and then she gave a crooked little smile and waved good-bye, teetering there on the icy slope. I tried to tell myself later that the smile was meant to tell me that she understood, that she was saying, "Go ahead. I know how tough it is down here at the bottom. If you can get out, go for it." I waved back, and she bent her head as if to concentrate on her footing, and I ran after the girls who had called to me.

After that Ruth and I didn't eat lunch together. I ate with the other girls. I don't know where she ate. I always made sure to say hi to her in the hallways or out on the playground, as if publicly demonstrating that I was brave enough to acknowledge I knew her, but she knew better. She'd just smile.

Of course I never really did come to belong within the tightly woven social structure of that small town but remained on the periphery, occasionally and randomly being included in one group or another. There were too many things against me: being a southerner and the daughter of a blue-collar worker, and my own propensity to be drawn to the eccentric and unusual characters—the outsiders—recognizing I suppose, kindred spirits.

But I never again turned my back on the unpopular or the disliked in the hopes of belonging as I did that day on Ruth. Even at nine I figured out that whoever you were with, you had to be able to live with yourself.

As a child I frequently heard my father say, "You always have a choice." This conviction was etched into my being from the beginning of my life by the heat of my father's hard-won certainty that each of us is responsible for our own choices. And life had given my father every excuse not to take responsibility. As a child he spent every evening in the lonely farmhouse that was his home, waiting for his father's return from a job in town at the furnace plant. He waited to see how drunk and angry his father would be, to see how badly he and his mother and his older sister would be beaten that night. My father would be the first to admit that there is a great deal we do not control, but he never used those years of abuse to justify or excuse any of his choices. Starting work at seventeen, married at twenty-two, and father of two children by the time he was twenty-five, my father worked hard, loved us deeply, and never abused us. His life was a decision to say, "I have a choice. The abuse stops here."

There's a great deal we don't control, but we always have a choice, if only in how we respond. I couldn't control the social rules and norms of small-town society. But I had a choice about how to respond, and I knew I'd made the wrong choice with Ruth. I don't tell this story with self-recrimination. I tell it because it's one of the stories in which I think I see myself most clearly. I see that when I am afraid I am not enough and want therefore to be a better than I am— want to be someone I imagine everyone will love so my belonging will be guaranteed—I make choices that run contrary to my own nature, hurting myself and others. This is no different at forty-six than it was at nine, although hopefully I am a little more self-aware if not any more courageous now than I was in fourth grade.

American Buddhist nun and teacher Pema Chödrön, in her books *Falling Apart* and *Start Where You Are,* talks about cultivating *maitri,* the ability to be an unconditional friend to the self, the basis of living with compassion and loving-kindness toward others. To be a good friend to the self we must be able, without harshness, to see the truth about ourselves, no matter how difficult or how beautiful this truth may be.

Of course all the news is not happy news. It's discouraging to realize how often not only do I not want to be who I really am, I don't even really want to be better than I am as much as I want to *appear* to be better. I tell a story about a famous speaker behaving badly at a conference I attended but then add a seemingly generous comment at the end about how it would be difficult for anyone with his level of fame and fortune not to get confused about being omniscient. I believe this is true, but if I were really being generous, if I really wanted to give him the benefit of the doubt, I simply would not tell the story. I add the corollary, not in any genuine outpouring of compassion for this man's pressured position in the limelight, but to make myself look less mean-spirited for having told the story in the first place.

Living awake is largely a process of increasing self-awareness so we can get out of the way and know the Mystery that is right there at our—in our—fingertips. It doesn't matter what you call it or how you do it—taking personal inventory and responsibility through a twelve-step program, cultivating the objective observer witness through meditation, developing the ability to stalk yourself daily by recapitulating your activities at the end of the day, or simply contemplating regularly the mystery of yourself and the world—it is the work of living a life centered in the soul. And the best way to avoid becoming narcissistically self-absorbed is to remember that the most profound and accurate self-knowledge is gained, not in isolation or under special circumstances, but by staying awake to our thoughts and feelings and actions during the fires of daily living.

Nathan, my younger son, and I are coming home from shopping, traveling by streetcar along the part of Queen Street that is lined with rundown shops and greasy diners offering the same daily specials week in and week out for the last ten years. It's hot, humid, and sticky, the kind of day that makes me want to move out of the city, the kind of day that makes us dependent upon air conditioning because we have cut down the trees that would have offered us cool green shelter and have covered everything with concrete and asphalt, which mirrors and multiplies the heat of the sun's rays. I'm tired and anxious to get home, attempting to remember to give up trying to pull away from the heat that is plastering my shirt to my skin with sweat as the streetcar stops and starts in the traffic, clanging its bell at cars that are double parked or making illegal left turns.

Suddenly, just as we seem to be picking up a little speed, I hear the streetcar driver shout, "Hey, what are you doing?" as the bell rings out once again and we stop abruptly. There's the sound of metal wheels squealing on metal tracks and a sad sickening thud. There's no mistaking that sound—the firm yet strangely soft and hollow sound of a vehicle hitting a body. The streetcar has struck a pedestrian.

People at the front of the streetcar are rising in their seats, their eyes wide. "Did you see that?" they murmur to each other. "He just walked right out in front of us. Driver didn't stand a chance." The driver is using his phone or radio to call for an ambulance. He gets off the streetcar and disappears.

Now, in situations like these I always feel like there is something I should do—not something everyone should do, something I in particular should do. I'm just not always sure what it is. My first-aid knowledge consists of a dim memory of learning to do the Heimlich maneuver years ago and repeatedly hearing my father, who regularly mangles or amputates small body parts while operating power tools, recite the mantra "apply direct pressure and elevate the wound." Unless the unfortunate individual we have struck has, in falling to the ground, inhaled chewing gum or a throat lozenge, the former would be unnecessary, and I am pretty sure the latter, if there is any bleeding, will be obvious to the transit driver or others more qualified to offer assistance than me. Generally, if I have no special skills to offer, I figure the best way to help is to stay out of the way.

The police arrive in record time. I once came home and found the front door of my house hanging on its hinges, clearly kicked in. Not knowing if the intruder was still inside, I called the police from a neighbor's and the patrol car arrived—from the station literally two blocks away—forty-five minutes later. Since there was no life at risk then as there is now, I suppose their sense of priorities is in fact quite appropriate. Along with the police, a small car with an ambulance service decal has arrived—not an actual ambulance but one man in a car.

The streetcar driver comes back on board and tells us all to get off. "We won't be going anywhere for quite a while," he says brusquely. We all obediently disembark by the rear doors, a few people grumbling about how they need to get somewhere, wanting to know how long this will take. But once we are out on the sidewalk where we can see the man lying in front of the streetcar, everyone grows silent.

It's hard to say how old he is. He is thin, and his skin hangs loosely on his bare arms beneath the torn T-shirt—fluorescent pink with the logo of some heavy-metal rock band emblazoned on the chest. His cheeks are caved in, and his face is flushed with a dark purple spider web of broken blood vessels beneath the gray stubble of a week's worth of growth. To what degree these are the ravages of time or simply the signs of life lived on the street with too little food and too much booze is hard to say. His pants are dirty and stained and too short. His dilapidated sneakers have no laces.

But it's his head I notice more than anything, the curve of his scalp beneath a few thin strands of gray hair, almost luminescently white in the bright sunlight, pale and fragile like a bird's egg there on the hot, dark pavement. A torn straw cowboy hat lies nearby, knocked off by the blow of the streetcar. I look at his chest. He doesn't appear to be breathing.

The police urge the crowd from the streetcar and those who are congregating from the surrounding buildings to stay on the sidewalk. The paramedic kneels down by the prostrate body and looks up at the crowd. "Does anyone here know CPR?" he calls out. Alone without a fully equipped ambulance, he is looking for someone to assist him. I want to say yes, even though it's been over twenty years since I took the course and can't remember any of it. I want to do something. He calls out his request again as he fits a mask over the man's face and begins squeezing the airbag and inflating the man's chest.

I want to step forward and say, "Show me what to do," but I am pretty sure that this is no time for a refresher course. No one in the crowd speaks, and I remember a story I heard once about some Scandinavian country where everyone—absolutely everyone—learns CPR. The death rate from heart attacks is virtually nil, and I wonder why we don't do this, why we teach our children skills like programming the VCR and coloring in maps of the world without going outside the lines but don't teach them a relatively simply skill that could save lives. The three cops are eyeing the crowd, hands on hips, and I wonder why they aren't assisting the paramedic. Don't all police officers learn CPR?

An ambulance pulls up, and two other paramedics join the one working on the still-inert form of the man on the street. You can feel a collective sigh from the crowd rise up into the hot air and hover there, like a small dense spasm of anxiety. We're off the hook. The experts are here. And they are working like crazy, pumping the man's lungs full of the thick city air, charging up electrical paddles. The streetcar driver is pacing in front of the crowd right along the curb, cell phone in hand. He is obviously talking to someone at the transit authority explaining how the man walked out of nowhere right into the streetcar, how he couldn't stop in time, how the police and ambulance are there now and traffic is backed up behind the scene for miles. His face is crimson, and he dabs at sweat with a handkerchief as he paces back and forth, puffing on a cigarette. I want to put out a hand and touch him on the arm and say, "It's okay; it wasn't your fault," but he is not close enough, and I wonder if this would help or just make him angrier or make him fall apart in a place where he would rather look busy and in charge. I wonder if he will go home tonight to someone who can be with him, someone who can let him rail on until the tears come.

The crowd, which to this point has been stunned into relative silence, begins to stir. Folks who don't know anyone speak into the air as if addressing a friend they wish were with them.

"Must have been drunk."

"He's in bad shape. Looks like he was in bad shape before he was hit."

"Ah, they'll patch him up."

A couple of people take to running commentary on the action before us as if the rest of us were blind, giving a blow-by-blow like radio sportscasters.

"There they go. They're going to shock him now and get the old ticker going again. There's three of them—one putting in an IV, one giving him air, and one charging up the paddles."

"Yup, there they go. Whoa! Did you see that body jump with the shock? Oh, here they go again. They're doing it again."

I want to tell them to shut up. But even as I have the thought, I realize that they can't, that they are talking to fill the space, to block out the silence of knowing that what we are watching is the death of a fellow human being. We are seeing the fragility and finiteness of our own lives.

Nathan looks over at me and mouths, "What should we do?" Suddenly he looks very young, and I realize that at fourteen he has never known anyone who has died, never seen anyone who was dying.

I move over and stand closer to him so our shoulders touch and say quietly, "He's not going to make it, Nath. Just watch. Say a prayer for him, and just be with him as he goes." We are watching a man's life end. You can almost see it, like a thin mist evaporating in the hot air, the life leaving this frail body. And as I say a prayer, I offer the only thing I have, my attention, to the ending of a life I know nothing about.

I wonder about that life. I wonder what he looked like as a little boy when his arms and legs were still firm and strong and his skin was smooth and pink. Did he laugh a lot? What did he dream of becoming? What did his mother dream for him when she held him as an infant? No doubt none of those dreams was of dying alone on the street after wandering out into traffic. The thought makes my breath catch, and I think, as I move even a little closer to Nathan despite the heat, "I am watching the death of some mother's son." I say a prayer for the baby and the boy he was, for his mother and her grief, wherever she is.

I wonder what path brought him here, who he made love to, whether or not there are grown children or young grandchildren out there somewhere who carried his DNA, people who might find themselves right now pausing for no known reason, feeling a strange tug, like a loose thread being pulled free and unraveling a small bit of knitting. Are they being touched by a strange sense of sadness or loss they cannot identify? Do they frown mystified and shrug it off with a shake of the head, moving to resume mowing the lawn or washing the dishes?

Or maybe there is no one. Maybe he was alone in his life. Maybe there is only us, total strangers brought to his death simply because we were on a particular streetcar. I want to go over and sit on the pavement and put his head—that fragile, white egg—into my lap, but I suspect the police and the paramedics would stop me, so I just stand there with my son while the crowd narrates the events and the paramedics gather up their tools. I just stand and pray for this man I do not know and will never know. I pray that he finds some ease in this passing, some peace that may have eluded him in life. And I do not look away as he leaves us.

On that hot afternoon in downtown Toronto, as in every other moment of my life, I have a choice. I couldn't save this man's life, and in the big picture—I mean the really Big Picture of the history of the cosmos or the planet or the species—it probably didn't matter if the man with the straw cowboy hat died there on the pavement or later at the hospital or in five years' time. Because the truth is that in the big picture the details of what happens to us and what we do or don't do don't matter, regardless of who we are. But I believe that *how* we live those details does matter. I'm sure the man on the road didn't know I was there, but I believe what I did—paying attention—made a difference, not necessarily to him, and not just because it made me feel useful, but because I believe that the big picture is somehow shaped by how we live the details, the little pictures that run through our lives. This is a belief I choose based on an intuition. It is not something I can claim to know. I can't really explain it, I certainly can't prove it, and I'm not trying to sell it. And I can't even guess how this works—how our choosing to be awake and keep our hearts open shapes the collective dream of the people or the planet or the cosmos. I just believe it does. So who I am is a woman who makes a choice to pay attention as often as she can.

### *Meditation for Being with Yourself*

This meditation is based on my experience with a small part of a wonderful larger Buddhist practice called *tonglen*, taught by Pema Chödrön. In tonglen I focus on receiving and sitting intimately with those feelings I usually try to get rid of and giving away—sharing with others—those feelings I generally try to hang on to, doing this first for myself, then for another, and finally for the world. I would highly recommend learning this practice.

Sit in a comfortable position, and bring your attention to your breath. Take three deep breaths in through your nose, breathing out through your mouth. On each exhale, inwardly tell yourself gently to "Let go." Let your shoulders fall a little. Let your weight drop down into your hips and legs. With each exhale, let go a little more. Feel your body rise and fall with your breath. Breathe into any place in your body where there is tension or tiredness, and on the exhale let the breath carry this tension or tiredness harmlessly into the ground.

As you continue to follow your breath, be aware of yourself and your surroundings. Be aware of any sensations you are having. Notice how your body feels, what sounds or smells or colors are around you. Neither resist nor focus on these sensations, but simply notice them. When thoughts come, notice them and let them go, gently bringing your attention back to your breath. Just be fully present with yourself.

Now let your mind review the events of the day—your interactions with others, your activities—lightly calling to mind how you have spent your day. Notice what feelings are evoked by these memories. Let yourself stay with these feelings, breathing them in, getting a little closer to the depth and breadth and color of each feeling. Notice which feelings you want to stay with and which feelings you want to push away. Stay with one feeling that is uncomfortable; choose one that is not overwhelmingly painful but simply uncomfortable. Be aware of any sense you have of trying to pull away from this feeling. Breathe into any places in your body or heart that resist this feeling, and let them soften a little in their resistance. Notice what happens.

As you breathe in a feeling you would normally want to get away from, breathe out a feeling you would usually want to hang onto, sharing it with others in the world.

Spend some time simply following the inhale and the exhale, sitting closer with a feeling you have found uncomfortable and sending out into the world a feeling you have tried to hang on to. As thoughts come, simply notice them and let them go. Notice without judgment what happens.

# FIVE

# *Choosing a Joyful Dance*

*Don't tell me how wonderful things will be . . . someday.*
*Show me you can risk being completely at peace,*
*truly okay with the way things are right now in this moment,*
*and again in the next and the next and the next . . .*

Here is the question: Are you willing to be completely at peace with how things are right now in your life? Are you willing for just one moment to let go of all your dissatisfaction, of all your suffering about how things are? Are you willing to let go of all the worry and tension in your body and simply breathe?

I think of happiness as the delight I have when I am aware of being completely at peace and fully present with myself and the world just the way it is in this moment. It is a lack of suffering plus a self-reflectivity that makes the peace I am feeling a conscious state of awareness. I am not simply at peace, I am aware that I am at peace—happy.

So, are you willing to be happy?

I'm not asking if you know *how* do this. I'm asking if you would be *willing* to do this if you knew how. It should be such a simple question. Who wouldn't be willing to be happy? But it raises all kinds of new questions that let us know why we might be reluctant to let go of our suffering. My thinking mind becomes suspicious: If I'm willing to be completely at peace with how things are in my life in this moment, does this mean the changes I long for will not be created? What about the things that *should* be changed—the ongoing polluting of the earth, the injustice in the world, my own self-destructive habits? Is asking me if I am willing to be happy with the way things are a way of trying to tell me things won't change for the better—my son will never find work he loves, I will never have a long-term intimate relationship with a primary partner or have stable vibrant health—so I may as well get used to the way things are?

My best friend, Linda, has been working in an organization that is slowly and painfully disintegrating. Her skills are ill used, unacknowledged, and undervalued. The daily atmosphere at work is poisonous to creative productivity, and changing the situation is not within her control. She knows she has to leave and is setting things in place to do so within the next few months. In the meantime it's hard for her not to get pulled into the daily machinations of office politics, worries about the future, frustration with how things are on the job.

Concerned for her health, I say to her, "Consider this for just a moment: Would you be willing to be truly okay with how things are at work today, to accept things just as they are, to let go of worrying and suffering over how or why they are not as you feel they should be or could be, simply to be at peace with what is?" Conflict and fear flash across her face.

"I'm afraid that if I am at peace with how things are I won't move to change things. I'll just get stuck there and won't leave."

"Why would you do that?" I ask, surprised. "You know it's not a good place for you to be."

"Because I'm basically lazy," Linda replies with a grimace.

"That's a pretty dim view of human beings," I say, smiling, "that we won't make the changes we need to make unless we are suffering because we are basically lazy."

Linda laughs. "Not human beings, just me. I'm lazy, not everyone else!"

"Aha, I see." We both laugh. Linda is one of the most industrious people I know.

I continue, "Not suffering over how things are at work isn't going to change what you know. You know it's not a good place for you to be. You want to leave because you know you can be more of who you are—can make a fuller contribution and have more fun—elsewhere. You're taking the actions necessary to leave. In the meantime, agonizing over what is wrong, railing internally or externally about injustices you cannot change, makes you miserable and exhausted. It doesn't speed the process up. In fact, it may slow things down by making you sick and tired. And it profoundly affects the quality of the only time you really know you have—this day, this present moment."

It is always so much easier to be wise and erudite about someone else's situation.

I do the same thing all the time: I confuse acceptance with acquiescence. I worry that peace will lead to stagnation. In the last few months of 1999 I found myself for the first time in many years truly at peace with living alone, my sons with me half of the time. Over the years, despite my deep satisfaction with my work and my relationships with friends and family, the ache for a partner has sometimes been a painful longing. The longing was still there, but it was no longer painful. I was not suffering over it. I felt a strange sense of peace, a new depth of appreciation for my life in the present moment. I was truly okay with being alone. This meant I had little or no inclination to spend time and energy dating, looking for a mate, or exploring relationships I intuitively knew were unlikely to lead to a long-term partnership. I felt a strange kind of trust that if a man I could share my life with crossed my path, I would recognize and move toward him. And I was okay if this happened tomorrow or in ten years. I was even okay if it never happened. Although I acknowledged the longing for deep intimacy with a primary partner, I was not suffering at all over being alone.

Except in the moments when I worried about being okay with being alone—moments when I was suffering over not suffering. I worried that I'd simply gotten too tired to care, had just given up. Was I accepting the present moment or cutting off possibilities because the known pleasures of a hot bath, good book, and restful night's sleep looked better to my middle-aged body, mind, and heart than the potential disappointment of a dinner date where the connection was at best tenuous and exploratory? Was I feeling content or hopeless? If I wasn't suffering over being alone, would I bother to go through those awkward first dates, the sometimes slow process of getting to know someone new, the self-revelation necessary to make a connection? Would I be willing to make the compromises necessary in any relationship, or would it all just seem like too much trouble?

Somewhere along the road many of us have picked up the belief that to change we must suffer. I remember talking with another workshop facilitator about sending out publicity for upcoming workshops and then waiting for registration. "I realize," she said, "that I feel obligated to worry about the registration, to agonize a little about what I will do if the workshop doesn't fill. When the workshop fills I am always secretly a little convinced that it is in part because I have worried; I've paid my dues for the success." We both laughed at the familiar and superstitious belief that rewards are earned with suffering.

Some things are earned with work. But work is not suffering. Work is just work. Sending out brochures for a workshop is work. Worrying about registration is suffering. Why would we believe that the latter has anything to do with the workshop's success? And why do we believe that we will not make the changes that are within our control and good for our lives—like Linda leaving her job or my making compromises in relationship—unless we are forced to do so by the suffering of job dissatisfaction or loneliness?

Years ago my family lived on the Welland Canal, where the large ships that sail the Great Lakes and the St. Lawrence Seaway move between Lake Erie and Lake Ontario. My father, who is not a strong swimmer himself, wanted us to learn to swim, wanted us to have a useful skill he had not had the opportunity to acquire. So when I was about six years old, he put a rope around my waist and threw me into the canal, reasoning that under such dramatic circumstances I would be motivated to swim. My father loves me. He really wanted me to learn to swim, and I am sure he thought this was the best way for me to learn. I was in not any actual danger of drowning; he could have pulled me out of the canal at any moment. But I was terrified. To a six-year-old child the high gray concrete wall of the canal looked unscalable and the dark cold water life threatening. I did not learn how to swim. I learned how to survive.

The first time I read the poem "The Swimming Lesson" from Mary Oliver's *New and Selected Poems,* it took me right back to the cold water of the Welland Canal and the hundreds of times since then that I have put myself in situations where I would either sink or swim, believing that it was the best way to learn.

## The Swimming Lesson

*Feeling the icy kick, the endless waves*
*Reaching around my life, I moved my arms*
*And coughed, and in the end saw land.*

*Somebody, I suppose,*
*Remembering the medieval maxim,*
*Had tossed me in,*
*Had wanted me to learn to swim,*

*Not knowing that none of us, who ever came back*
*From that long lonely fall and frenzied rising,*
*Ever learned anything at all*
*About swimming, but only*
*How to put off, one by one,*
*Dreams and pity, love and grace,—*
*How to survive in any place.*

—*Mary Oliver*

When we believe that we are by our very nature deeply flawed—self-indulgent, selfish, judgmental, sinful—our efforts to fulfill our soul's longing to live fully become efforts to control, chastise, reshape, improve, and change ourselves. Believing we are by nature lazy and unworthy, we believe we will not change, will not become the people we want to be unless we are pushed or forced by suffering to do so. Given this belief, we use methods that do not cultivate mercy and compassion for ourselves but rather foster a hardness toward our own suffering and the suffering of others who are failing to curb or rise above their basic nature. And in the face of these methods we do not learn to swim or dance or dream or be all we are. We do not really learn to love fully or allow ourselves to receive love freely. We're too busy surviving.

In the poem "It Felt Love," translated by Daniel Ladinsky in *The Gift: Poems by Hafiz the Great Sufi Master*, the fourteenth-century poet Hafiz talks about another way of learning, a way based on the assumption that to grow is to reveal the innate beauty we hold within, a beauty best brought forward by tender encouragement.

## It Felt Love

*How*
*Did the rose*
*Ever open its heart*

*And give to this world*
*All its*
*Beauty?*

*It felt the encouragement of light*
*Against its*
*Being,*

*Otherwise,*
*We all remain*

*Too*

*Frightened.*

*—Hafiz*

If we believed that we were by our very nature compassionate, gentle, and capable of being fully present, our task—living our soul's longing for deep intimacy—would be a matter of finding and placing ourselves within the warmth of the internal and external "encouragement of light" in our lives so we would open and open and open to all we are. I am not suggesting that this is easy, especially for those of us who have spent a lifetime surviving the sink-or-swim school of self-improvement. Often we don't even know where these lights of encouragement are in our lives.

For several years I have facilitated a writing group that met in my home every second week. I have been in writing groups that are a virtual feeding frenzy of criticism. Group members are expected to contribute by tearing to shreds the writing efforts of others. No one I know who has participated in such a group has written more than they would have if they had simply stayed home. Many have given up writing altogether as a result of attending such groups. So our group has one very clear rule: you have to ask for the feedback you want. One young woman new to the group picked up on the essence of the rule right away. Just before she read the first draft of a raw personal story about her mother, she paused and said, "I only want to hear the good stuff right now. This is too new and too personal for anything else, so only tell me what you like about it." So we told her the good stuff. We told her about the parts we liked, the parts that moved us to tears or laugher or insight. Several weeks later she reread the piece, asking for feedback on more technical matters of structure and coherence, which the group was able to provide for her.

It's amazing to me, given that so many of us are sink-or-swim veterans, how quickly most people who join the group figure out that what they want—what they need if they are to become better writers—is feedback that encourages them by telling them what pieces moved and touched the listeners and why. And let's face it, after weeks of no one mentioning how inspired or amused or touched they were by that technique you love so much where you make everything analogous to eating ice cream or playing baseball, it just kind of falls by the wayside. The ineffective writing falls away, and the powerful writing grows deeper, gets better.

But once in a while someone responds to all this support with suspicion, like it's some kind of trick to get them to drop their guard and take a big breath just as they're about to be doused with the bucket of ice cold water they knew was coming all along. It's understandable, really, and the fact that it doesn't happen more often is probably good evidence that we are by our very nature gentle and compassionate beings who move naturally toward the light of encouragement. When you're not used to it, encouragement can be frightening in its unfamiliarity, can make you feel much more vulnerable than the harsh criticism you know you can take because you have survived it over and over again.

Last year a wonderful writer, Jan, came into the group and then left after three sessions. She told me on the phone, "Well, the people in the group seem very nice, but I'm not sure they can give me the tough feedback I need." I suggested that she try asking for the specific feedback she wanted, although I admit that on occasion, if I suspect the feedback someone is asking for will tear at some precious piece of themselves, I, as the group facilitator, will intervene and suggest an alternative approach. But what became clear was that Jan simply did not believe that encouragement would work. She truly believed that the only thing that would make her writing better was harsh criticism of what was wrong with it.

Sometimes it's so much easier to believe the bad stuff that we don't even want to hear the good stuff. We are afraid that all that is holding us together is the armor we've put on to survive what is hard. We are afraid that if we lay down the armor and open ourselves to that light of encouragement—really receive its warmth—we'll simply fall apart and be an embarrassing puddle on the floor. Jan couldn't risk it right now, and I didn't push her. Pushing wouldn't have helped.

I myself have been an advocate of the sink-or-swim school of learning. The teacher I chose, the medicine man with whom I apprenticed, was a real sink-or-swimmer if there ever was one. He'd been a U.S. Marine! He gave me my medicine name, Mountain Dreamer, and told me it means one who always looks for and pushes the edge. But over time "the edge" has changed. At some point it occurred to me that pushing the edge for some of us was not about doing more or trying harder or going further or faster but about doing less, trying easier. This changed my teaching.

For the first few years of leading vision quests—ceremonial time where individuals fast and pray alone in the wilderness—I would urge participants to go as far from the base camp where I would be as they could. I wanted them to get the most out of the experience. Many of them had been raised in large cities, so the wilderness at night with all of its unknowns was a truly frightening place. Still they would venture valiantly forth, spending a good deal of their solo time terrified of chipmunks that sound like foraging bears when it's dark, frightened of getting lost or eaten or carried off by God knows what. The only good thing I could say about this is that their fear kept them awake—that and the swarms of mosquitoes and blackflies.

But one year all that changed. I changed. I said to the group that was going out, "It doesn't matter how far you go. If you want to stay where you can see my tent all night, that's up to you and fine with me. Explore. Go out and then come back. Try out different places and see what feels right for you. Find a place where you feel you can do what you came here to do. It doesn't matter to me, and I can't imagine that it matters to Spirit exactly where you do your praying. If you need to be afraid, fear will come wherever you are, but you don't need to go out looking for it."

Two things happened. First, the majority of the group went farther into the wilderness than they ever had during the years when I was urging them to go beyond where they were comfortable. The freedom to choose, the encouragement to trust themselves, gave them courage.

The second thing that happened was that a few people who were not at all used to being away from the lights and sounds of the city chose places that were in fact within sight of my tent. Freed from the fear that would have totally preoccupied them had they been elsewhere, and in some cases had overwhelmed them in previous years, they were able to be fully present with their own prayers in a way they could not have been had they ventured farther, motivated by my well-intentioned go-for-it mantra.

Over time, all these experiences have slowly softened my heart and opened my mind to the possibility that what the Grandmother in the dream is telling me now is true—we only have to become what we truly are.

Lately, when I do my daily practice I find myself praying to live gracefully. I have a very particular feeling in my body when I remember or imagine a graceful day. It is a day without rush, a day when I am not suffering over things not being any different than they are, a day when I take a breath and accept those things I cannot change, like long lineups in the bank or traffic jams or the weather. It's a day when I rest easy in a mysterious knowing that there is enough—enough time and money and energy and heart in the world and in my life, a day when I know that I am enough. It is a day when I am simply present with myself and all that is around me. It is a day of being truly happy, of feeling graceful—comfortable in my own skin and life.

To dance is to move gracefully. To live our soul's longing is to be willing to live grace-filled moments. Grace is the opportunity to be happy that *we do not earn*. That's what makes it grace. But if we are old-time sink-or-swimmers, if we believe that our basic nature is in need of fundamental renovation, the unearned gifts of grace make us nervous. They stir feelings of guilt and fears about potential envy; they heighten our sense of unworthiness and enmesh us in a sense of obligation to work harder at being the people we feel we *should* be. If we are not in some essential way a manifestation of the Mystery that bestows grace, grace can feel like yet another burden.

To dance, to move gracefully, to receive the grace-filled moments every day, we have to know that we are worthy not because of our hard work or our suffering or our eagerness to be other than we are; we are worthy by our very nature—the same nature that creates and sustains all that is. When we know this we are able to answer the question "Are you willing to be happy?" with a quiet but confident, "Yes."

### *Meditation on Worthiness*

The two phrases "I deserve . . ." and "I am deserving of . . ." have very different connotations. The former indicates something I feel owed because I have earned it with hard work or suffering. When I say "I deserve a rest," there is a sense that I am calling attention to something I have accomplished, some effort I have expended that has now earned me a rest. It may be complaining at the lack of an earned rest or demanding a rest as a deserving reward for my efforts.

The latter, "I am deserving of . . . ," rather than being a justification or complaint or demand, describes something about me that is reflected in an aspect of life either currently present or about to be created simply because I am worthy of it. When I say, "I am deserving of rest," I feel something inside me let go of the notion that I must earn a rest. My perspective shifts toward seeing myself as someone who by virtue of my very existence and nature is worthy of rest, as are all others.

Sit with paper and pen in a comfortable position. Now, picking up your pen and paper, write the phrase "I deserve. . . ." and complete it on the page. When you have finished one sentence, repeat the phrase and complete it again, over and over for five full minutes. Write without censoring or judging what you are writing. No one else will see it if you do not want to share it. If nothing comes, simply wait, repeating the phrase until you can complete it again. When five minutes have passed, put your pen down.

Now, close your eyes if you are comfortable. Take three deep breaths in through your nose, and exhale through your mouth, letting your shoulders drop on the exhale. Breathe into any places in your body that are tense, releasing with the exhale all stress and tiredness. Spend a few moments focusing on your breath, following the inhale and the exhale, the rise and fall of your body. If thoughts come, acknowledge them as thinking and allow them to drift away, returning your attention to your breath.

Now, once again, picking up your pen and paper, allow the phrase "I am deserving of . . ." to come to your mind. Write it down and complete it on the page, over and over again for five full minutes. If nothing comes, simply wait, repeating the phrase slowly until you can complete it once again. At the end of five minutes return once again to following your breath and clearing your mind.

Now, look at your two lists. Which is longer? Was one phrase more difficult to complete than the other? Read them out loud. Is your tone of voice different when you read one list than the other? What happens if you take the phrases from the first list and preface them with "I am deserving of . . ." instead of "I deserve . . ."? Just observe your feelings without judgment, and stay with them. There is no right or wrong way to do this. We are seeking self-knowledge, not self-judgment.

# SIX

# *Hitting the Wall*

*I have heard enough warrior stories of heroic daring.*
*Tell me how you crumble when you hit the wall,*
*the place you cannot go beyond by the strength of your own will.*
*What carries you to the other side of that wall,*
*to the fragile beauty of your own humanness?*

There is a difference between being the determiner in your life and being the controller. We often confuse the two. The desire to control is a normal human response to fear. The ability to determine is the ability to remember who and what you are—that you are in your essential nature compassionate because you are an embodiment of the Great Mystery—and to act from the center of this awareness.

There's a great deal we do not control—the weather, other people, often our own thoughts and feelings, to mention only a few. This is the reality of life lived as a human being. Everything changes. Everything that lives dies. These are truths, whether we acknowledge them or not. And part of me is glad—glad that there are things that are true whether I have the courage to believe or remember them or not. When I hear a spiritual teacher announce that she will never have arthritis or a stroke or a brain aneurysm because she will simply never allow the thought-form to be in her consciousness, I wonder what she thinks is going to happen eventually. I mean, sooner or later, unless you are planning to live forever or spontaneously evaporate—both highly unlikely and not necessarily desirable in my mind—something is going to go; some part of the body will begin to break down as death approaches. This is the reality of our mortality, and how we deal with that reality—whether we deny it or can be with it and the fear or acceptance or relief it evokes within us (depending on how well things are going on a particular day)—tells us something about how we deal with the multitude of things that are not within our control. When we look our own mortality in the eye, one way or another, we deal with the limits of our own power. And there are limits.

I know this isn't a popular view right now. Workshops with titles like "Tap into Your Own Infinite Power" and "Develop the Personal Power to Create Anything You Want" draw huge crowds. Understandable, really; the world is a wild and woolly place, and you'd have to be slightly crazy not to be occasionally afraid for yourself or your children or the planet. And the human response to fear is to want to get things under control, and power seems to promise us control.

But what about the places where we hit the wall, the places we cannot go beyond by the strength of our own will no matter how many workshops we attend, no matter how serious our intent? There are different kinds of walls; addictions, compulsions, obsessions, mind-numbing depression, and heartrending grief are just a few. The wall is the place where you find yourself in a puddle of tears in the middle of your kitchen floor, and the only words that come are "I can't."

When I read the many journals I have kept over the years I despair at the number of times I have resolved to slow down, do less, live at a more sustainable pace. I mean, it's endless—pages and pages of resolutions and accounts of canceling plans, pulling back, lowering expectations, reprioritizing, and reorganizing. I get tired just reading it! And clearly it hasn't worked, since there it is, again and again and again, the same weariness, the same overextension and resolve to change, often inspired by periods of illness brought on by simply doing too much. I read the entries and finally in exasperation slam the books shut and say out loud, "Oh, for heaven's sake, Oriah, give it up! You clearly can't do it!"

And for the first time I get it. I—particularly the *I* that feels driven to do more and more—really *can't* slow down. If I could, I would have.

Some of the people who have taught me the most in my life are recovering addicts, usually incredibly strong-willed people, all of whom have hit the wall of their own limitations with a bone-cracking and often life-threatening crunch. And the road of recovery—living a life where the substance or behavior to which they are addicted is no longer determining their actions—always involves the difficult and continuous acknowledgment that they simply cannot, by their will alone, change the behavior that was destroying their life. And so they hand their addiction and their lives over to that which is larger than themselves, that which they name God or truth or love or even the community upon which they rely.

So I follow their example. I hand over that aspect of self that is driven to do more and more to the sacred presence that has always been with me. Most days I do this prayer in a way that acknowledges that I am handing over the driven aspect of self—that aspect that forgets that she is enough—to the Mystery that is both larger than myself and embodied within me. I ask the part of me that the elders who are my teachers call my Hokkshideh, the part of me, however small, that remembers who and what I am, to direct and care for my Shideh, the aspect of self that in its fear and forgetting feels it must do more and more and more.

Some days I do my prayer gently, some days I do it desperately, often I do it repeatedly throughout the day. And then I try to act in accordance with my prayer. If I ask the Mystery to lift this drivenness from me and then schedule ten appointments in the day, I have to question the seriousness of my intent.

For a while, when I did this prayer an image would come to mind, a picture of a couple of hamsters—cartoon hamsters, Chip and Dale without the stripes—on one of those exercise wheels they put in hamster cages. These hamsters were inside me, somewhere around my navel, actually, and they couldn't get off the wheel. They just kept running and running and running, not getting anywhere, clearly exhausted but unable to stop. I'd imagine this hand reaching inside me and gently scooping the hamsters out of that wheel and setting them down somewhere. I have a vivid imagination that does not lack a sense of humor. Some days the hamsters would just lie where they were put down, panting, their small pink tongues hanging out, their eyes closed. But other days, they'd recoup quickly and sit up or start walking around, exploring quietly. Some days they'd even dance.

This visualization worked as a place to start, in part because it was so comical. Becoming seriously driven about changing the drivenness was not likely to be a step in the right direction. The visualization also steered me away from being harsh and judgmental toward the aspect of self that is driven; the hand wasn't punishing the hamsters but giving them a much-needed respite.

But at a certain point I realized the humorous nature of the image was, in part, a defense against facing the seriousness of my compulsion to do too much. It was a little like an alcoholic who jokes about last night's drinking spree. I was hedging, not really getting it. There were too many payoffs to not getting it—the admiration of others in a culture that values productivity above all else, periodic guilt-free time alone because of headaches or exhaustion, and, most important, a sense of being able to stay one step ahead of a small black dog snapping at my heels, the demons whispering, "Not enough, not enough."

Sooner or later when we surrender what we cannot control we have to hold still and let the demons we have been running from catch us. There is no greater terror. But there can be no greater liberation than to face those demons held in the arms of your own compassionate nature and that which is larger than yourself. I can't tell you it's over. I'm still doing it, every day—handing the driven aspect of me over to what is larger than myself, sometimes with a prayer as simple as "Help me" when I find myself heading to check my e-mails before I have eaten or barreling toward a sixteen-hour work day. And I sit still and face the demons and breathe and let my own compassionate essence gently redirect the aspect of self that is lost, that has forgotten once again that she does not have to earn her place by doing things perfectly or working harder.

One of the traditional Native American ceremonies I have participated in and led is called an Eagle Dance. An Eagle Dance is a prayer for the self and the world spoken through the movement of the body. The rigors of the dance mean that at some point it becomes for the dancers a microcosm of the places in our lives where we hit the wall, the place we cannot go beyond through our will. The ceremony is difficult to the degree that a dancer insists on trying to go beyond this wall by the strength of his or her own will alone.

We start at dawn and end at dusk. Participants have spent three days doing meditation, prayer, and purification ceremonies to focus their intent for the dance. They can consume no food or water for the day of the dance and can take only one or two five-minute rest breaks with the permission of the leader. The dancers blow eagle whistles, which send out a shrill cry as they run toward the central tree, which represents the sacred center of life that sustains us, and dance back to their places on the circle again and again, never turning their backs to the tree. They move to the rhythm of the drummers and singers, who support them with prayers in song.

My job when I am leading is to keep people dancing, knowing that if they can keep themselves in the dance, that which can carry them beyond the pain or fear or hopelessness they cannot overcome on their own will find them. At some point in the dance almost every dancer—hopefully not all at the same time—hates me, feels I am somehow *making* them do the dance, pushing them more than others or deliberately ignoring their request for a break. I don't take it personally. When we hit the wall of our own limitations, one of our first reactions is to look around for someone else to blame.

Lynn is a beautiful, intelligent, talented woman who, much to the bafflement of those around her, often feels that she has less to contribute to the world than others. She has been working on a doctoral degree for several years, and it is now time to write her thesis. She is lost, daunted by the size of the task and no longer sure she has something to say or a right to say it.

As the dance progresses past midafternoon I can see Lynn struggling to continue, slowing down, adjusting her skirt or her belt or her whistle between runs to the tree—anything to avoid continuing. When we encounter what we cannot control we resist continuing. We look for distractions—and life is full of them—ways to turn away from the wall we are approaching, to postpone the inevitable recognition of our limitations. Finally Lynn goes down on one knee and stays there. I go to her place on the circle, kneel beside her, and ask her what is happening.

"I want a drink of water," she says without raising her head.

"You can't have one." I keep my tone matter-of-fact.

"Fuck off!" She keeps her head down but glances at me sideways to gauge the effect of her words and continues. "I've had enough. I want to get in my car and go find a Holiday Inn."

I wait a minute and speak again, careful to keep my tone neutral. If I step in too close to her, she will collapse. If I am harsh, she will run. I feel an ache in my chest for her, for me, for our certainty that it is too hard, that it will always be hard. I long for her to find that which is both within her and larger than her, that which can carry her and teach her that it does not have to be so hard. But I cannot give this to her. I can only help her stay where it can find her.

"Lynn, here is the truth. If you head for your car no one here is going to tackle you on the way to the parking lot. It's completely up to you. But you and I both know you have been here a thousand times in your life—right here, where you are three-quarters of the way through, and you can't see any way to go on, and you can't see the other side, and you just want to quit. And you can. No one is going to stop you. Or you can try something different. You can go to the tree, one more time."

"You don't mean that. It's a long way until dusk. It's not *one* more run to the tree, it's a *thousand* more. And I can't do it!"

"No, I do mean it. There is no other way to do it. Make one run to the tree. That's all you have to do. One more. And if you try anything else—if you try to do a thousand or a hundred or ten more—you will not be able to do it." I know that if she cannot stay in the present, cannot ask for help with just this run to the tree and only this one, just this next step—the one her foot is taking right now in the only moment we ever really have, the present—she will not be able to continue.

Something in her believes me. Or maybe she can't remember where she left her car keys. Or perhaps she wants to do something different. Slowly she gets to her feet, puts her whistle into her mouth, and moves toward the tree in the center of the circle, one step at a time. Over the next few hours she does not falter, although I can see the struggle on her face at times. She keeps going to the tree. Two years later when she puts her five-hundred-page thesis—written one page at a time—into my arms like a precious child she has birthed, we laugh and remember the Eagle Dance together.

John is also in the dance. John is a gentle, openhearted man who worries most of the time in almost all situations about what could go wrong. And John has a wonderful imagination; he can conjure up all the possibilities. As a result he has suffered for years almost constantly with a variety of anxiety-produced ailments—headaches, backaches, stomach upsets, the list is endless. I move to his place on the circle as he abruptly and unceremoniously sits down. He's on his way to lying down, a position from which it will be difficult to get him up and going again. When I squat next to him and ask what is happening, he responds in short gasps, clearly finding it difficult to breathe.

"I have terrible pain," he says, leaning back on one elbow. "My joints, my chest, my head . . . everything hurts . . . I don't see how I can continue."

I stay where I am, silent for a moment. I know John well enough to know that this is a place he often finds himself—overwhelmed by excruciating yet not life-threatening physical pain that is induced by his anxiety. I reach over and put my hand gently on his chest. His heartbeat is strong and steady. *"John,"* I say softly but emphatically, *"you are not the pain."* His eyes fill with tears, and sobs begin to wrack his body. When we hit the wall of our limitations we are often so overwhelmed with the pain or the disappointment or the fear that we forget that these are not who or what we are. They are so large within us that they block out our awareness of all else.

"John, I don't want you to stop crying. I don't want you to ignore the pain. I just want you to stand up and go to the tree, the way you are."

"I . . . I don't . . . know if I can." The words come out as a soft wail past the sobs that continue to shake his thin frame.

"You can if you don't try to move away from the tears and the pain. You can if you remember that you are not the pain, not the anxiety. You can if you pray and let something larger than yourself take you as you are to the tree one more time. Go slowly, but go."

John gets up, still crying and shaking. I move away, and he starts for the tree one more time. A half hour later I am amazed to see him gently but enthusiastically going to the tree—clearly renewed and no longer in pain.

Later John and I talk about his anxiety and all the years he has spent seeking to be free of the pain it causes him.

"John, here's the problem: you think that at one of these ceremonies or in one of our sessions together either I am going to say something, or you are going to see something, or something is going to happen, and the lightbulb will go on and you will know how to get rid of your anxiety forever." John grins and nods in agreement. I pause and slow my words down. *"It is never going to happen."* He looks at me, surprised.

"This anxiety that plagues you is not within your control. You cannot change it with your will. Don't you think that if it was within the control of your will to get rid of this anxiety that you would have done it years ago?" Tears begin to make thin wet lines on John's face. "I know this is hard. But look at what is. I don't think you are masochistic, do you?"

"No."

"And of course there are times when you get attention because of the illnesses the anxiety creates, but do you really think this is a big enough payoff that you would want, even unconsciously, to continue to be plagued with this anxiety?"

"No," he says again.

"I'm not saying that there isn't a great deal in this up to you. The trouble is that when something has been with us as long as the anxiety has been with you, it becomes so familiar it's habitual. But I know you want to be free of it, or at least not have it running your life and making you ill so much of the time. If you could change it with your will you would have already done so."

"So what do I do?" he asks, bewildered.

"Hand it over to something larger than yourself," I say. "Every single day, every moment if you have to, offer a prayer that says, 'Here I am. I can't do this on my own. I do not have anxiety. It has me, and I hand it over to that which is larger than myself—to the Great Mystery, to the power of Love, which is the life force of creation.' Do it any way you want, but say, 'Help me.' "

"But why do I have all this anxiety? It doesn't make sense."

I can feel his mind struggling for a way to handle the anxiety, to understand it out of existence.

"It's doesn't matter why, John. And the truth is you may never know because it's probably a combination of a thousand things—genetics, conditioning, habit, past trauma . . . who knows? You still believe that if you can figure out why, you can control it. But the truth is, I'm not sure you can ever completely know why. You've spent a lot of time looking, and you've gained some insights, but has the anxiety gone away?" He shakes his head glumly.

I sigh and laugh a little. "John, I can see by the way you look at me that you don't believe me, and that's okay. But I honestly believe that you will not be free of this anxiety until you face the fact that it is not within the control of your will." I pause, my throat suddenly closing with the emotion of wanting this for him. "And, John, you're almost fifty. I would wish for you something different for the rest of your life."

We have developed technology that has extended the power of our will over the external environment beyond our ancestors' wildest dreams. Perhaps this is what makes it hard for us to believe that some things, including some internal states that determine the quality of our lives, are beyond the control of our will. Over and over again I watch myself and others refuse to ask for the help we need from that which is both larger than ourselves and part of our essential nature. Caught in our addiction or compulsion, riddled with anxiety, or driven to work harder, we cannot even see the truth of who we are. Opening ourselves to the beauty that is around and within us even when we are in pain, paying attention and surrendering what we cannot control to who this beauty, this Mystery, keeps telling us we are— now that's an act of power.

## *Meditation of Surrender*

In this meditation I have focused on simply letting go of the trying and hanging on we are sometimes not even aware we are doing. I have included after this meditation two prayers. One is a general prayer in which we surrender that aspect of self that forgets its true nature and becomes frightened to the presence that is larger than ourselves and is at the same time our true nature. The other is a prayer surrendering a specific aspect of self—using my own drivenness as an example—that we have found we cannot control with our will alone. Obviously the particulars of this latter prayer and the language by which you name that which is larger than yourself can be adapted to your own needs and preferences.

Sit or lie in a comfortable position, closing your eyes if you are comfortable with that. Take three deep breaths in through your nose, and exhale through your mouth, letting your shoulders drop on the exhale. Breathe into any places in your body that need attention, letting any tiredness or tension leave with the exhale.

Bring your attention to your breath, and take a few minutes to simply focus on the exhale and the inhale. Be aware of the sounds or scents around you, bringing your attention back to the inhale and the exhale with each breath. Notice the rising and the falling of your body. If thoughts come, just notice them and let them drift away with the exhale like clouds crossing the sky.

Focus for a moment on your body—on any places in your body where you are holding on. Let go. Send your breath into any places where there is tension, and on the exhale let your body soften. Do this repeatedly, with each exhale feeling yourself more and more supported by the surface under you and the earth beneath this surface.

From this place of relaxation, softly repeat and complete the statements, "I surrender . . . ," "I let go of . . . ," and "I quit trying . . . ," letting the completions come without judgment or censorship. Notice without judgment how you feel as you complete the statements. How does your body respond? Just stay with any feelings or sensations that come as you repeat the statements, noticing what happens within yourself. If tension arises, take a few moments to breathe once again into any places where you are holding on in your body, releasing the tension with the exhale. Allow yourself enough time to stay with each statement, waiting for the completion to arise from a deeper place within yourself.

*Great Mystery, hear my prayer. I surrender my will—my actions and my thoughts on this day—to my own compassionate nature, to that aspect of self that does not forget that it is you I embody in my essence. Guide me in this that I may feel your presence and remember who I am, that I may serve that to which I belong, the Sacred Mystery that is life.*

*Sacred Mystery, see this one Oriah Mountain Dreamer. I hand over to you that aspect of self that is driven, that pushes to do more than my body can sustain. Hold this aspect of me, hold my fear, with compassion that I may remember all that I am and know it is enough.*

# SEVEN

# *Dancing Together*

*And after we have shown each other how we have set and kept
the clear, healthy boundaries that help us live side by side with
   each other,
let us risk remembering that we never stop silently loving
those we once loved out loud.*

We think we choose who we love. But I think we simply do the best
we can to be with each other where love—the Mystery that sustains
us—claims us.

A life where there is love is often messy. Life without love is
neater, but neatness is really preferable only in bathrooms and written reports. Dancing alone is often easier and certainly less compli-
cated than dancing with someone else, but there is nothing quite so
satisfying as creating even one moment of real beauty moving gracefully with another. Perhaps to find this beauty more often, these
moments of moving in exquisite alignment with each other and with
the music that guides us, we need to let go of our ideas of what the
dance should look like and let the messiness of love guide us.

My exhusband, Des, the father of my two sons, Brendan and Nathan, is getting married today. We have been apart for thirteen years. I live in townhouse #16, Des lives in #2 at the other end of the courtyard. While the proximity is not entirely comfortable for either of us, this arrangement has made it easy for our sons to go back and forth between the two households.

This is the dance of separated coparents, of two people who are at times painfully aware of the ongoing connection they will always have through the children they love even though they have ceased to be friends or lovers or mates. We are cautiously courteous with each other and have had remarkably little conflict when working out schedules, although both of us, contrary to all we intend and believe to be wise, occasionally grumble to our sons and friends about insignificant and probably imagined slights perpetrated by the other. Previously mutual friends see only one of us, custody having been determined at the time of separation. Our sons, having no such option, justifiably tell us both that they do not want to hear our complaints.

Brendan and Nathan, now nineteen and sixteen, are clearly excited about the wedding. They come over to my place to show me their new suits. Shoulder-shrugging boys are transformed into handsome, responsible young men by dark blue wool, starched white collars, and crimson neckties.

Nathan asks me to help him practice his duties as usher for the ceremony. I instruct him to step forward, introduce himself with a simple, "Hi, I'm Nathan, Des's son," and hold out his arm asking, "May I show you to your seat?"

In his nervousness he cannot get it right. "Hi, I'm Nathanson," he stumbles, jutting his arm out in front of me as if he is directing traffic or holding back an angry mob at a demonstration. His older brother's burst of laughter does not help. He eyes widen in panic. "What am I going to do?" he wails. "Help me, Mom."

"Just relax," I say, trying to sound calm and supportive while biting my bottom lip to stop from laughing. "You're the host. All you have to do is focus on the people coming in, on putting them at ease."

"But what if a woman doesn't take my arm, doesn't know what to do, or gets mad?"

"Just push her up against the wall and tell her, 'Hey, baby, take this arm or no seat for you!'" his brother suggests helpfully. I give Brendan a warning look even as I laugh.

"Nathan, don't worry. If a woman ignores your arm and marches through, just let her go or walk alongside. You don't have to give her a nosebleed with your elbow."

"Just grab her and pull her down the aisle, whether she wants to go or not," Brendan quips.

I know in part where Nathan's fear comes from. He has heard me tell the story of a wedding I attended years ago where another young man was nervously offering his arm to women entering the church, his face flushed with tension, his voice skidding between octaves and cracking uncontrollably. Two women I knew, both in their late thirties, were ahead of my partner and me. The young man, clearly uncomfortable but determined to do the job he had been given, stepped forward and, extending his elbow slightly, asked, "May I show you to your seat?"

The woman closest to him turned and glared. "I think I can manage to walk down the aisle without your help!" she announced in a booming voice. "Women are not cripples, you know!"

People already seated turned in their pews to see what the commotion was about. The young man turned a darker, impossible shade of scarlet and looked about desperately, clearly unaware of how he had offended. I moved up quickly beside him and slipped my hand into the crook of his elbow. His arm, thin beneath the grown-up jacket, trembled slightly. "I would be very happy to have you show me to my seat," I said, smiling at him reassuringly. Confused but clearly relieved at having something to do, he escorted me down the aisle.

Later, I spoke privately with the woman. "I don't understand what you were doing," I told her. "Did you really think you were striking a blow for women by humiliating that young man publicly for doing what he had been told, for trying to be courteous to you? Did you really think he was suggesting that you looked too fragile to make it to your seat? And what do you think he will remember from this? To honor the feminine or to be wary of women who might, without any warning or immediate cause, want to lop off his balls?"

She had no response. I could have told her that I too have been afraid of being trapped in old confining roles, have in my anger struck out at the wrong person. But this was years before I had discovered the breadth and depth of compassion. I thought I had to choose sides. I didn't know that compassion could tenderly hold both her anger and fear and the young man's embarrassment.

I know Nathan is remembering this story now as he prepares to be usher at his father's wedding. He understands about five thousand years of patriarchy. He knows about misogynist culture and does not want to impede women's struggle for liberation. But mostly, like all sixteen-year-old boys—like all of us—he just wants to do a good job and avoid public humiliation.

So we practice ushering over and over.

Later, when he and Brendan come home, stumbling in at midnight full of stories and intoxicated by having been so close to the center of attention and by their first real imbibing of alcohol, Nathan will tell me the ushering went fine. "There was," he will tell me in a tone of shared confidences, "one girl about fourteen who was really nervous. She said to me, 'I don't really know what I'm supposed to do.' But I just told her, 'That's okay. I do, I'll show you,' and I put her hand in my arm and took her to her seat."

He will be glowing with a quiet pride, his confidence in his ability to do what most men want to do—to offer something of value and meaning to the women around them—having grown this evening. Too late for my marriage with his father, I figured out how important this is to men. It wasn't that I didn't appreciate their father's caring when it was there, but my dogged—one could say doctrinaire—independence left little room for him to feel there was anything of real value he could offer to me that would be fully received.

Brendan prepares for the wedding in a different way. Being the official "best man," a fact he cannot resist mentioning repeatedly with emphasis to his younger brother, he has decided two hours before the ceremony that he wants to offer a toast at the reception.

"Help me," he says as I am repeatedly ushered by Nathan across the living room. "I need a poem, something good."

"You want to read one of my poems at your father's wedding?" I ask with feigned innocence. I can't help but take a moment's pleasure from this idea. After all, I knew the groom—intimately—and the bride, Bonnie, had been a very close friend of mine when Des and I were married.

"No," he says, exasperated. "Not one of yours. That would be tacky. One by someone else. You know thousands of poems. You must have one. I don't have time to look. I want to recite it, not read it. I need it fast so I can memorize it, and I only have two hours."

Showing remarkable restraint, I do not point out that he has had days, if not weeks, to prepare for this, that this is supposed to be my Saturday alone, that I have work if not a life to attend to, and that it is at least a little weird for me to be finding a poem for a toast at my exhusband's wedding. I don't really want to have anything to do with this. It has nothing to do with me. But it is happening in their lives, and so it is happening in mine. Love is what links us to events in the world no matter how remote they may seem. It can make it difficult to stay clear about where I end and others begin. There is a thin line between life-sustaining interconnectedness and life-draining enmeshment.

"Okay," I say. "Let me think."

But I don't have to think, nor do I have the time. I know the perfect poem for a wedding, the one I would have read at mine if it were today. Only later do I realize that offering it here will make it awkward to use at any possible ceremony of my own. But for now I am focused on Brendan's need. I pull out David Whyte's "The TrueLove" from his book of poetry, *The House of Belonging*.

Brendan reads it. "This is perfect! Can you write it up on the computer and paste it on cards the way you do for the poems you use at workshops?" I hesitate, feeling myself being more drawn into this than I want. "Please. It will take me forever."

So I type, print, cut, and paste. Brendan reappears with a sheaf of papers in hand. He has a role in the ceremony offering some opening prayers. "Can you go over my speech and the rest of the stuff I have to say in the ceremony with me?"

Almost against my will, drawn by a curiosity I suspect of being both morbid and self-abusive as well as a genuine desire to give Brendan confidence on this day, I start to read the sheets. They are the text for the whole ceremony: Brendan's prayers, the welcoming of the guests, Des's and Bonnie's vows. I wince. I know I should not read this, but it is too late now. I cannot stop.

They have written their own vows—simple, heartfelt promises to love and support each other through good times and bad, even when they are disappointed in each other. That is the part I will remember most clearly—the acknowledgment that disappointing each other is unavoidable and the commitment to love when the inevitable happens.

Reading the words, I feel a strange sinking sensation, as if the floor is moving, not dropping away suddenly, leaving me suspended midair, but slowly sagging and taking me with it. The memory of another wedding twenty years ago flashes through me—no dress, no ring, no customized vows or circle of friends. Des had gone to work that morning, not wanting to lose a day's pay, and I had gone to classes. We had two friends present as witnesses there in city hall. We were young. We'd been living together five years. Marriage, in our minds, was an archaic institution. We were going through the motions for the tax man. We didn't think the legalities or the ceremony mattered. What mattered was our relationship, our commitment to each other.

We were right. And we were wrong.

Distracted, I turn back to the pages. For the first time it occurs to me that Bonnie and Des actually love each other and want to make a life together, the way Des and I did so many years ago. How could I not have known this? They have been together, although not sharing a home, for over ten years. They are getting married.

A burst of laughter at the magnitude of my own blindness escapes from my mouth like a gasp, and Brendan looks at me warily, perhaps sensing the weirdness of the situation and wondering if I am about to flip out and cease to be useful in the process. But there's no time to contemplate the depth and breadth of my denial. I help Brendan reword the prayers he has to say and type up the new version. Then he reads me his speech. He welcomes Bonnie into the family and talks about how he is glad she is marrying his father both because he likes her and because her presence helps him get to know his father better, joking about how three guys in a household exchange minimal personal information at the end of a day when there's no woman around to encourage expansion upon "How was your day?"

"Fine. Yours?"

"Fine."

"Good."

Later that night, sitting on the side of my bed, he will tell me how everyone cried during his speech and recitation of the poem and came up to him later to tell him how beautiful it was. "Even people who weren't there told me when they came later that they'd heard I had made a wonderful speech," he will say, glowing. "People asked me for copies of it, said it was the high point of the evening." I will be proud and happy for him, pleased to see how good he feels. He has been feeling lost, as so many of us were at nineteen. Floundering at school, afraid to move into his own life, he hasn't enjoyed many successes lately.

As I listen to him now rehearsing his speech, I see the man he is becoming. I give him the asked-for pointers on emphasis and wording. Both he and Nathan go to help their dad load the car but return moments later with anxious pleas for me to teach them to dance. Twelve minutes to departure, and they want me to teach them how to dance!

I know it's hopeless, but I put on some music—"I Heard It Through the Grapevine" by Marvin Gaye from *The Big Chill* CD. They object but concede its appropriateness when I point out that Des and Bonnie are the same age as I am—old—so they are likely to play *old* music at the wedding.

Brendan is hopeless. I try to show him a basic step. We all end up laughing so hard we can hardly stand, so I give up and tell him just to close his eyes and see if he can find the rhythm—any rhythm—and if so, just to bounce up and down slightly on the spot.

Nathan has dance potential. He lives in much closer proximity to his body than his brother. But he is also much more introverted and unlikely to dance. It doesn't really matter. There's no time anyway. In a flurry of brushing lint from jackets and last-minute mirror inspections, they are gone.

And I am alone. I am not aware of being upset. I don't think I am. But I feel oddly unable to decide what to do next. I sit down at the kitchen table for a minute. Twenty minutes later I am still sitting there. Tasha, my cat, cries for food and rubs up against my leg, bringing me out of my reverie with an involuntary shudder.

We have been separated for over a decade without any hope or desire for reconciliation. What is there still between Des and me, between me and anyone with whom I have loved and lived, sleeping curled in each other's dreams? Whatever it is, it is not static but changing, the ground of my being feeling the tremor of this new marriage. It was naive not to expect it, and I am strangely pleased that I am, after all these years, capable of such innocence, happy to learn I am not continually anticipating the past in my present. And yet my unpreparedness makes me feel that I have been broadsided, an old ache aroused by an unanticipated blow.

Bonnie moves into Des's townhouse. I feel confused about living in such close proximity to the newlyweds even as my mind argues that it should make no difference. Mail for Bonnie is accidentally delivered to my townhouse. I hear that the women of the townhouse complex are holding a welcoming party for Bonnie, and I am, understandably, not invited. When I telephone my sons, her voice is on the answering machine announcing that this is the home of Des, Bonnie, Brendan, and Nathan. No one else seems to think I should be bothered by any of this, so I give my feelings no room. And the truth is, I don't know what I am feeling. I feel no animosity toward Bonnie, but something, some knowledge I have hidden from myself, has been aroused from its slumber by the shift in circumstances and is stalking me. There is nothing I can do, but I wait for it to pounce and reveal itself.

And it does. One morning I wake up hearing my own voice echo from the dream. "I'm hurt." I lie there feeling stunned and stupid like someone who has to have a very obvious joke explained to them. Why would I be hurt?

But I am. To my shame and horror I discover I have never forgiven Des for emotionally leaving the marriage years before I walked out the door. And I discover that I, who have always thought of myself as not having a vengeful bone in my body, wanted him to pay for this by living alone, hopefully full of regret and presumably pining away for me every day for the rest of his life. How dare he remarry? How dare he be happy?

I am embarrassed by all of this. I know better. I have done therapy. I have a spiritual life. I have believed and told others with sanctimonious certainty that forgiveness is a natural state that simply comes with time. Des and I have been apart for thirteen years! There was no abuse, were no beatings during the marriage, just two people under the normal stresses of a young family who failed to take care of the relationship at the center of that family. I *know* this, and yet here I am, devoid of the forgiveness I have glibly assumed I had generously bestowed years ago.

I am lost. Knowing what I need to do, being aware of what has been left undone, may be an essential step in the process, but I do not know how to proceed from here. How do I take care of the hurt, which, no matter how irrational, is an ache at the center of my life? How do I let go of the anger I know is not enhancing my life and truly forgive myself and my exhusband for the pain we caused each other years ago?

Stymied, I meditate and pray. A question comes: What do I know about looking after a physical wound? It has to be protected, tended. Pain tells us something needs our attention. And so I focus on the hurt during my meditation, softening to the ache, just trying to hold myself in my own heart without judging myself for still feeling the hurt, for not having forgiven completely. I do not try to rid myself of the hurt but simply try to be with it, to move closer to it. And the hurt begins to ease a little.

Then early one evening, about six months after the wedding, Brendan calls to tell me that Bonnie is in the hospital. They have discovered that Bonnie has several holes in an artery in her back. Blood is putting pressure on her spinal cord. It is a rare condition that has to be treated. Surgical intervention will repair the leak but holds a high risk of rendering her paralyzed from the waist down, confined to a wheelchair.

I go over to Des's house the next morning to pick up Nathan. Des descends the stairs looking like a man who has not slept all night. I can't help but think how much worse we look at forty-five when we lose sleep than we did at twenty-five. "How are you doing?" I ask him.

"Well, I've been better." He tries to shrug nonchalantly, but his eyes widen around the edges. Ah, how well we know those we have loved. Even after all this time I recognize the gesture as one he uses to ward off tears.

"Des, I am so sorry. If there is anything I can do for you or Bonnie with the boys . . . getting groceries . . . driving . . . anything . . ." He pauses, and I watch the slow crumble begin. Nathan is watching from the stairs. My words surprise even me: "I love you . . . and Bonnie. . . . I would do anything I could to help."

I know as I say it that it is true, and I can see in his eyes that he knows it also. He starts to cry and leans toward me, collapsing for a moment into his own fear. We hug briefly. We have not touched each other in thirteen years. These bodies, once so familiar, are strangers to each other and yet not completely so. How could they be after all those years of leaning into each other—while I gave birth to our sons, when Des's father died, during lovemaking and sleeping and dancing and laughing and crying together?

All this flashes through me in an instant as if the contact between us completes a circuit that runs a video of body memories held at a cellular level, and I wonder if we are every truly separated from those we have loved, those we have cared for and hurt. It only lasts a moment. I do not want to be the one who causes a crack in his will to be strong because I know I am not the one who can help him through this new terror, even though I may understand its roots more than most. Our marriage did not survive the incredible pressure of my years of illness and disability from chronic fatigue immune deficiency syndrome. And now, only six months after marriage to another, he faces the possibility of her being permanently disabled. He must be terrified, mystified, angry at the gods.

And I? As I go through my day I let myself remember the young woman who was my friend so many years ago. We had worked together for several years in a small two-person office coordinating social justice groups for an international student organization. We were pregnant at the same time. I was at her labor for the birth of her daughter, Molly. I sat with her as she wept when she and Molly's father separated. We had not been friends for some months before Des and I split up. Her craziness of that time—a hard time—had worn me out, and my judgment of her craziness had sent her away.

I cannot help but wonder how this must be for her, knowing that this could be the very last week of her life when she can walk across a room, dance to music, or simply feel warm bathwater on her legs. Is she savoring every moment, fully conscious and aware of those simple movements we all take for granted after we've graduated from our first teetering steps as an infant? I think of her as I rise from my chair in the kitchen to refill my cup with tea—effortlessly moving across the floor, standing by the stove. I wonder if my kitchen, identical to the one in her new home with Des, is big enough for a wheelchair. I wonder if the countertop and stove elements are easily accessible from a sitting position. Surely the water taps must be too far away. I pull a chair over to the sink, sit down, and reach over toward the taps. Awkward, but I can turn them off and on from here.

This is not my story, and yet I am deeply affected by how it shapes the lives of my sons and a man and a woman I discover on some level I have never stopped loving. And as I realize this, the hurt I had buried for years and recently learned to treat with tenderness begins to dissolve. It is a relief to recognize that our lives are woven together, that each is truly another myself. I let go of trying to understand the why of the weaving, of trying to untangle the knots that bind us together. Oh, the healthy boundaries that govern our regular contact stay clear, but I let go of pretending that we are not all part of the same story, a story we cannot entirely see or understand. I let myself remember us all as we were twenty years ago—friends and lovers—and I am content to pray for each of them and for myself, all of us just human beings doing the best we can, bound to each other as surely as we are bound to breath and blood.

Bonnie undergoes three operations. The last one results in the predicted paralysis. Now, months later, with rigorous daily physiotherapy, sensation is slowly returning and she is learning to walk again, graduating from wheelchair to walker to canes. She does not know if she will ever walk unaided again, but we are all hopeful.

It is life that teaches us about our incredible capacity to be compassionate, to be with what is, to love ourselves and each other and the world. And for most of us, most of the time it does not happen in the grand causes and revolutionary changes. It happens in the small things, in our human struggles in relationship. As we learn to trust our essentially compassionate nature and our capacity to love, we do not have to guard against this love; we know we can keep the boundaries that help us live side by side, and we know that we truly never stop loving, however silently, those we once loved out loud. And we are renewed by the wonder of how love carries us beyond where we thought we could go.

## Meditation for Those We Once Loved Out Loud

Sit or lie down in a comfortable position. Breathe three deep breaths in through your nose and out through your mouth, letting your weight drop down with each exhale. Bring your attention to your breath, breathing into any places in your body that are tired or tense, releasing with the exhale. Follow the rising and the falling of your body, relaxing more deeply with each breath. If thoughts come, simply let them go, and return your attention to your breath, following the movement of air in and out of your body.

Breathe into your heart. Imagine your heart expanding slowly, relaxing and softening in any of the places where there is hardness. Feel the endless capacity of your heart to expand.

Now let someone you once loved come to mind. Let it be someone you have not seen or spoken to in a long time. It may be someone who has died or someone who is still living. Let your heart remember how you loved this person. Can you remember good times together? Painful times? How you met? How you parted? Do not reach for particular memories, but see which ones come when you simply focus on the love you felt for this person.

Be aware of whatever other feelings come with these memories—sadness, hurt, anger, regret, grief, happiness. . . . Whatever the feelings are, simply notice them. Is there any fear in remembering that you once loved this person? Any regret? Whatever the feelings, breathe them in, sitting closer and closer to them. Can you soften your heart to whatever feelings come? Without judgment, simply be with the love and any other feelings the memory of this person evokes.

Think now of someone else you once loved. Again, let it be someone you have not seen or talked to for some time. Once again, breathe in whatever feelings accompany your memories of this person, sitting with them. When you have some sense of receiving all that you can in this moment, invite the image of yet another person you once loved to come into your heart's memory.

Be aware of all these places love has taken you. Be aware of how despite the fact that other feelings—of pain or regret or fear or sadness—may block the awareness of loving another, the connection between us and those we have loved never completely dissolves. Breathe into the knowledge of these connections, knowing that this holds no risk to you—that it is sometimes appropriate and always possible to remove ourselves from each other's circles without casting those we have loved out of our hearts. Feel the freedom this gives us to acknowledge the love we have for another without fear of losing ourselves or putting ourselves at risk of being harmed. Be aware of how this great capacity of the heart is yours. Breathe into your heart, and feel its expansiveness.

# EIGHT

# *Dancing on the Earth*

*Take me to the places on the earth that teach you how to dance,*
*the places where you can risk letting the world break your heart,*
*and I will take you to the places where the earth beneath my feet*
*and the stars overhead make my heart whole again and again.*

Writing about the places on the earth that restore my heart and feed my soul is like telling you the prayers I say when no one else is listening, like sharing the whispered conversations my lover and I have late at night after the lovemaking has washed our hearts clean. I fear you will dismiss me as a romantic, a tree hugger. And I confess, I have hugged a few trees over the years, have pressed my body along their strength and felt the tremor that runs through them when the branches a hundred feet above are tossed in the wind while the roots stay loyal to the ground that gives them life. The body learns what the eye cannot see—that even when they appear to be standing still, inside the trees are dancing.

I have been avoiding writing this chapter, rewriting the ones before and skipping to the ones that come after. I keep getting up and making tea or going for a walk or taking a nap—anything to avoid writing. I even tried changing the piece of the prose poem that begins this chapter. It refused to go. I don't want to write about nature. I never read so-called nature writing, unless we count Mary Oliver's poetry. She just gives you what she sees around her. She's not trying to sell you real estate or faith in the restorative power of the earth or camping equipment. She's just paying attention. And that's what makes things holy. Perhaps I am afraid I won't give to the places that are holy to me the attention they deserve. Or perhaps I am afraid that I will.

This kind of resistance deserves some consideration. There is some truth here, just below the surface, that will require something of me if I tell it to you now. That's the thing about truth; it changes us, requires us to live differently.

A year ago a friend gave me an astrological reading for my birthday. The astrologer told me, "You need to go to places this year where your body and heart feel lush." Good advice whether you believe in astrology as a useful tool or not. I've been thinking of it ever since, talking to others and hearing about their favorite island paradises and oceanfront resorts. Understandably, many Canadians tend to equate "lush" with "warm." And all the while I keep telling myself and others that I don't know where these places are for me.

And that's lie. A lie I tell myself so I will not feel the pain of the longing for these places.

All I have to do is think of where I want to go—where I am pulled as if by some horizontal gravity—when I am wounded. When I am hurting the way an animal hurts—without thought, without understanding, wild with grief—there is only one impulse: to go north, to drive away from Toronto, the city where I live, to travel through the rolling hills and farmlands of southern Ontario into the wilderness of the north where I grew up. And it is not until I see the massive rocky outcroppings of the Canadian Shield, the ancient pink and gray glacial granite heaving its shoulders out of the soft earth, that my animal body feels it is at home.

I was nineteen when I moved to the city to go to college. For a long time I couldn't stand to go to a park downtown or a conservation area just outside the city. Their manicured lawns and noisy crowds only intensified the ache I felt to be in the wilderness. They were a pale imitation, a mockery of what my heart and body needed. It felt easier not to open the longing. So I sought solace in those things the city does offer—the theater and classes and people I love—and buried my need for the inaccessible wilderness.

But once in a while something unearths my longing for the wilderness—an image, a story, a piece of poetry—touching me unexpectedly and making me gasp with the depth of the ache. Even now, knowing what it will say, I cannot recite Susan Griffin's prose poem "This Earth, What She Is to Me" from *Woman and Nature: The Roaring Inside Her*, without feeling my heart break a little. She ends the piece:

> This earth is my sister. I love her daily grace, her silent daring and how loved I am. How we admire this strength in each other, all that we have lost, all that we have suffered, all that we know; we are stunned by this Beauty, and I do not forget what she is to me, what I am to her.

Sometimes we decide to bury a longing that seems impossible to fulfill because we cannot bear the pain. The danger in doing so is that we forget the name of that longing. And if we cannot find it again, we lose a piece of ourselves.

Once, years ago, I counseled an unhappy woman. Over several sessions Sarah told me of her dissatisfaction with her life—her loneliness, her struggle with overeating, her desire for a mate, for a child, for work that would satisfy. Her gestures were heavy, her face was tired and sad.

Then one day she told me about a trip she had taken two years earlier to Israel, birthplace of her parents. As she spoke it was as if she had been illuminated by a light from within. She described the city of Jerusalem where she had lived for three months, how she had loved the noise and the chaos, the people shouting impatiently in lineups at the bank, the strange and magical mix of ancient traditions and modern life. She told me about the desert—the sky on fire at sunset, the sand like liquid gold, the stark beauty that made her want to get up at dawn and stare transfixed at the landscape. She was transformed by simply talking about it.

"Sarah," I said to her, "I have never seen you like this. Clearly this place is your home, the place your soul longs to be. Why are you living here? Why aren't you living in Israel?"

Her face closed at the question, and she spoke firmly as if shutting a door someone had carelessly left open. "That's not possible. There are too many problems."

I was dumbfounded. "What problems? Sarah, I'm sure there would be difficulties, but in all the time I have known you I have never heard you speak of anything that so clearly makes you happy. Your face is absolutely radiant when you speak of this place and how you feel there. There is nothing to keep you here. Whatever problems there are surely would be worth overcoming to have this kind of joy in your life, to be where you know you belong."

"I can't," she said, choking back tears. "You don't understand.

There are no available men in Israel. Single women outnumber men four to one. If I live there I will never marry and have a family." She wiped her eyes roughly and swallowed hard. "That's just the way it is."

Nothing I said could persuade Sarah that there was any way for her to live in the place she loved, that her chances of building a life of joy—alone or with a partner—were best where the person she was would shine, regardless of the possible accuracy of any statistical odds. That was ten years ago. Recently I met Sarah walking along the street. Past childbearing age, still single and looking weary and unhappy, she told me she was still living in Toronto. I did not have the heart to ask if she had ever been back to Israel, if she had ever gone home.

Facilitating workshops and retreats, I have heard literally thousands of prayers in circles, in sweat lodges, in healings and ceremonies. I have heard prayers of gratitude and requests for relief from physical and emotional pain, for mates and money and knowledge and direction. I have heard men's prayers and women's prayers, the prayers of Buddhists and Christians and Jews and Hindus and Muslims, of Wiccans and Shamans and Pagans and those who do not identify with any group or tradition. And beneath all the differences in language, all the variations in the specific human needs of the moment, I always hear the same prayer, the same ache of the human soul. At the end of one such circle, after hearing the prayers of the human hearts around me echoing my own, I said very softly, "We all just want to go home." And the men and women around me wept.

I once heard Edgar Mitchell, the Apollo astronaut who went to the moon and later founded the Institute for Noetic Sciences, speak at a conference. He was talking about new discoveries in quantum physics. The information was well documented and clearly articulated, but I remember little of it. What I remember is one line he said when telling the story of how he came to be interested in the study of meta-physics and meaning. He was describing the Apollo mission, how they had had some time off during the return trip to the moon, had been able to spend some time just thinking and looking out the space shuttle portal. What he said was, "When we turned around and headed for home, I had some time to myself."

It was the phrase "headed for home" that shook me, that made something inside ache a little. We say we are headed for home when we are out for the day and headed back to the building in which we live. We say we are headed for home when we travel, meaning we are going back to the country where we live and perhaps were born. But when Edgar Mitchell said they were "headed for home" he was not referring to his house or his hometown or to the United States. He was referring to the planet Earth, and I heard what space travel had given him, could give us all even if we never leave the Earth's surface: a clear sense of how this small green and blue planet whirling about in an infinite universe truly is our home.

We are all lost without this sense of home. And it is easy, living in cities where the ground is covered in concrete and the trees are planted in boxes, to forget that the earth beneath our feet is the same earth as that of the wilderness. Home is, of course, not simply a phys-ical place. It is a sense of belonging, of remembering and being re-membered, put back together again when our journeys into the world have fractured and fragmented our sense of self. But we are physical beings. Our bodies are made of the same stuff as the rest of the uni-verse and gravitate to specific places on the earth where this belong-ing is felt at a cellular level.

I don't know why different places on the earth speak specifically to different people. Over time I have come to appreciate the beauty of a variety of places: the subtle colors of the desert, the rolling swell of the ocean, the lush fertility of farmland and orchards, even the throbbing excitement and creativity of New York City. But none of these is home to my body and soul the way the wilderness of northern Ontario is. There is something about the starkness there that gives me comfort. The harshness—the unforgiving angle of the rocks, the sharp bite of the cold—is not personal. It simply is. It defies my desire to soften the edges of life. It is raw and plain in its beauty, relentless in its randomness. There is a strange solace in how small its immensity makes me feel, power that inspires awe and cultivates necessary humility when I or my people forget there are forces we cannot tame or control. The wilderness is where I meet life as it is, as others meet it at the ocean or in the mountains or on the plains. The ageless rocks shift and transform, their hardness yielding to the softness of wind and water over eons, whether I notice or not, whether I ever write about it or not, whether I see them as a metaphor or am content to let a rock be a rock.

I do not know why, but I do believe that for each of us there is at least one place on the earth where our hearts and our bodies are mended and renewed. We need to find and go to these places if we are to learn how to dance. Living in the city, I tried to cut off this need to avoid feeling the pain of having it unmet. And I became very, very ill.

It wasn't just being in the city that made me ill, but when I was diagnosed with chronic fatigue immune deficiency syndrome I knew I would have to find some way of getting myself back to the wilderness. I had become entrained to the pace of the city, a pace that was burning my heart and body up from the inside out. With no money to buy land up north and an illness that made camping with two small children increasingly difficult, I saw no way to find time in the wilderness.

Then one weekend my friend Linda invited me up to a trailer she had just bought on a campsite a couple of hours north of the city. Despite her reassurances that the site was isolated, I was wary. The very idea of trailer camping conjured an image of bumper-to-bumper trailers in an overcrowded field, the sound of radios blaring over the whirling buzz of the neighbors' blender mixing mai tais.

But this site was different. One of ten sites spread around a large spring-fed lake, it was in the middle of eighty square miles of undeveloped wilderness. I arrived at the site before Linda and took her canoe out onto the lake. And there, in the center of the lake, I lay down in the bottom of the canoe and let myself drift and cry and pray. I knew I needed a place exactly like this—needed it immediately— and I did not have the time or the energy or the money to even look for such a place. I had waited too long, had kept the longing, the knowledge of where my body and heart could be repaired, at bay for too many years. I was out of time. A solution seemed impossible, but I let my prayer for the impossible go out anyway.

And three weeks later the site that had been Linda's was mine. Linda, in her infinite generosity and love, bought the more expensive adjacent site, which I could not afford, so I could purchase her original site. She probably saved my life. For the next seven years on weekends and for the ten weeks of the summer I would spend my time alone or with my sons there in the wilderness, gaining strength in my body and healing for my heart.

How can we recognize the places that teach us how to dance? By the way they let us sit still. When I am in the northern wilderness I can effortlessly do the one thing I cannot do anywhere else: absolutely nothing. At the trailer site, whether there alone or with my sons, I would rise each morning and make a cup of tea and go down to the tiny wooden dock. And I would sit and stare at the water, waiting for the sun to spread its warmth over the land, drinking my tea and doing absolutely nothing for a very long time. No planning, no thinking, no talking . . . just looking and breathing and sipping tea.

And sometimes, after hours or days or weeks of doing nothing, after my body had received some invisible strength from the rocks and the water and wind, I would begin to notice things. I would hear the gentle plop of the otter's body entering the water and see his dark gleaming head, fur slicked back and bright eyes above the water in between long smooth dives. I would hear the merganser duck with her strange red-spiked headdress—the punk rocker of ducks—calling to her babies to keep up as she paddled along the shore, ever wary of fox and other predators. And when these creatures and the others with whom I shared this spot on the earth—bears and wolves and owls—began to swim or walk or fly within feet of me, I knew then that I was once again becoming part of the landscape from which I had been separated, that the smell and feel of things that were not me were being washed from me.

To live deeper we have to go to the places that help us find a slower rhythm. But simply going to these places is not enough. We have to let these places touch us, change us, speak to us.

Years ago a friend of mine organized a trip to Africa for a group of high-profile authors and motivational speakers from North America. These men and women were leaders in the field of personal growth and spiritual development. Many of them had developed models that sought to challenge traditional corporate perspectives and bring the language of soul-filled living to the business sector. The trip was an opportunity for them to meet and talk with traditional tribal elders about the needs of the people on the planet at this time.

It did not go well. On the first night in camp they built a fire and waited. When the tribal elders and their translator arrived, they sat together around the fire. The North Americans began to ask questions about the land and the people, and the elders reluctantly and briefly responded. And then they left.

On the second night, when the elders came and sat by the fire, the visitors from Canada and the United States again asked some questions, and again the elders responded with brief one- or two-word answers. After a while the North Americans gave up. While the elders sat, they made small talk among themselves, went to their tents, made tea, or cut wood for the fire. And the elders left, returning to their homes for the night.

On the third night, feeling frustrated and impatient, one of the men from the United States, who was widely known and revered for his development of a five-step process to facilitate meaningful dialogue, decided to take charge. Through the interpreter he explained his process to the elders and proposed that they begin the work for which they had journeyed so far. The elders spoke among themselves for a moment, clearly disturbed by this suggestion.

Finally the translator spoke. "The elders do not understand. They thought you came to have a dialogue with them about the needs of the people. But each night they come and there are questions and people moving about doing things and now this plan you propose. They do not understand how you expect to be able to talk with each other if you cannot be quiet together and listen to the earth. If people cannot hear the earth, how can they expect to hear one another?"

Sitting in silence, slowing down together to listen to and actually hear the earth, was not a part of the visiting North Americans' models or experience.

Going to a place on the earth that speaks to us is not enough. We have to able to listen with the very cells of our being to truly receive what the place has to offer to us. But if you can listen, what you will hear is the truth you may have forgotten, the truth that lets you sit still, the truth that who you are is enough. Of course you are still yourself. Don't expect someone better, someone saner or more insightful or miraculously and infinitely wiser, to suddenly occupy your body no matter where you are. Wherever you go you take who you are, your particular human foibles and peculiarities, with you.

Once when I was alone at my trailer site, I spent an afternoon lying on a blanket beneath the cedars and the hemlocks, alternately closing my eyes and dozing and gazing up through the branches at a sky so blue it hurt to look at it. Suddenly there was a sound, as if the air itself had begun to throb. It was like the pulsing of a soft but powerful engine, growing stronger, louder and closer with each beat. My chest constricted in fear as I opened my eyes and looked up. I could not imagine what it could be. It was above me and coming closer. My mind flashed on a conversation I had had the day before about UFOs. As a skeptic I'd been complaining that if another civilization had the intelligence to master space travel, you'd think that once in a while, simply by the law of averages, they'd abduct someone we all knew to be sane. Now, afraid and unable to identify the strange sound above me, I watched my mind go from the improbable to the ridiculous: maybe they'd heard me and were coming for me now, and no one would believe me, either. God knows I am hardly the paragon of sanity and stability: two divorces, alternative health and spiritual practices some might find suspect, and clearly an imagination completely out of control. I thought of calling out, "I didn't mean *me!* I meant someone everyone would know was telling the truth. Like Ann Landers or Doctor Spock—the pediatrician, not the Star Trek guy—or Oprah. . . ."

You see what happens? No matter where you go on the planet, no matter how calming or centering or renewing the spot is for you, you still have to take yourself along. This is important to remember. There I was, peaceful and calm and renewed on the land that is home for me, and my mind was still wild and woolly and full of bizarre twists and turns.

With visions of extraterrestrials racing through my mind, I raised my head from the ground just in time to see two great blue herons fly directly overhead, not more than five feet above me, their huge wings beating the air in a slow rhythm as they swooped down to land in the water on the other side of the tiny bay in front of me. They took my breath away—the power in those bodies, the grace and ease of flight, the sound of movement so majestic it made me feel small and happy.

Changes in my life resulted in the choice to let the trailer site go several years ago. For twenty-six years I have lived in a large city, and for the last four years I have not had a place of my own to go to in the wilderness. And the truth that I knew I would have to face in writing this chapter—the truth I wanted to avoid because it necessitates change and risk—is that my time is almost up. Some part of me is holding on by her fingernails, waiting for my sons to move into their own lives so I can return to the land that sustains me. I do not regret living in the city. I would neither leave my sons nor take them from their father. These are the choices we make. But inside, I am pacing myself to last throughout my younger son's final two years of high school, and then I will go to back to the land that knows me.

This is what home is: not only the place you remember, but the place that remembers you, even if you have never been there before, the place that holds some essential piece of you in trust, waiting for you to return when you go out into other places in the world, as you must.

## *Meditation for the Places You Are Remembered*

This meditation involves writing. You can do it without writing, but for me the attention to detail is easier to find and capture when I write it down.

Sit in a comfortable position with a pen and paper nearby, and let your eyes close. Breathe three deep breaths in through your nose and out through your mouth, letting your shoulders drop on the exhale, letting the weight of your body drop down into your hips and legs. Be aware of the surface you are sitting on, of the floor beneath this surface, and the earth farther below, supporting you. Bring your attention to your breath, following the inhale and the exhale for a few moments as they enter and leave your body. If thoughts come, acknowledge them and gently let them go on the exhale, returning your attention to your breath.

Now allow the phrase "I am going home" to enter your mind, and see yourself journeying—by car, on foot, by plane—to a place, a natural setting somewhere on the earth. It may be a place you know well, or it may be someplace you have never been. Suspend the judging mind, the thinking mind that would evaluate the practicalities of getting there or being there. If a place does not come to mind immediately, just let yourself wander and journey in your imagination repeating the phrase "I am going home." Be with any feelings that come, but resist the urge to consciously pick a place to alleviate the tension of perhaps not knowing where home is for you. Take all the time you need.

If a place comes to mind, see yourself there in your imagination. If a place does not assert itself in your imagination as the place you are seeking, even after patiently sitting with it for a while, choose a place you know to be pleasant with the intent of exploring what qualities of home this place has for you.

Give yourself time to imagine the details of this place. What time of day is it? What season? Notice the temperature, the colors around you, the scent in the air. When you are ready, pick up your pen and paper and begin to write a description of this place. Be as specific as you can: What kind of vegetation is there? What sounds do you hear in this place? Are you alone, or are there other humans around? Are there animals or birds? Let your hand move on the page without censorship or judgment. Include in your physical description of the place your experience of it. What makes it feel like home? What is the sensation of belonging? How does your body feel, your heart, your mind and spirit?

When you feel your description is complete, read it through and sit once again with your eyes closed, imagining being in the place you have described. Be aware of any thoughts or feelings that arise. Let the thoughts go, and simply sit with the feelings.

# NINE

# The Choreography

*Show me how you take care of business*
*without letting business determine who you are.*
*When the children are fed but still the voices within and around us*
*shout that soul's desires have too high a price,*
*let us remind each other that it is never about the money.*

We make choices about how to take care of business, how to make sure we take care of our needs and the needs of our children. The question is whether or not we can let the song of our soul—our essential nature—guide those choices when fear is singing in our other ear. The question is which tune do we dance to, which piper do we pay.

Many years ago I facilitated groups for women who were in abusive relationships. Some were married, some were not. For some, leaving meant walking away with the clothes on their backs, with absolutely no money, and with children to support. Others, if they left, would walk away with fifty percent of assets valued at several hundred thousand dollars. And everyone—without exception and regardless of their circumstances—talked about financial concerns as the primary reason they were hesitant to leave. What became apparent in the more than twenty groups I ran over a five-year period was that although finances might influence exactly when a woman left and certainly shaped to some degree how she left, money or the lack of it was never the reason she stayed. When women were ready to go, when they felt they really were worthy of something better, when their desire for a life free from violence was greater than their absolute terror of being alone for the rest of their lives, they walked out the door with whatever they had—empty pockets or accumulated assets and regular support payments, an inadequate monthly welfare check, a minimum-wage job, or a blossoming career. It was never really about the money.

Which is not to say that the money—the means by which we exchange our energy for what is needed to care for ourselves and our children—does not have to be taken care of. It does.

As an idealistic teenager mulling over choices about future work and relationships, I would passionately proclaim, "Money doesn't matter!"

To which my father, a hardworking lineman who provided for his family, would reply, "Money doesn't matter so long as you have enough of it." For my father, *enough* did not mean extravagant wealth—although our modest three-bedroom home, used car, three square meals a day, and warm clothing would have looked like wealth to a great deal of the world's population. *Enough* to my father meant the amount it took to take care of the immediate needs of his family. As adults, we need to know we can take care of this business.

Divorced with two small children, I decided fifteen years ago to do what I love and value—teaching, writing, and counseling focused on spirituality—and to do it in a way that allowed me to be home when my children returned from school at the end of the day because this was important to me. This meant running my own small business out of my home. I did not expect this choice to be rewarded with boundless prosperity in some kind of cosmic deal. I sat down and figured out how to get people to pay me for doing what I wanted to do. I set my fees by figuring out how much work I could do in a year and how much my sons and I needed to live on, with an eye to what people like me could afford and what was generally being charged for the kind of thing I offered. I refused to go into debt even when things were tight. When we wanted things beyond the basic necessities—like a car or a vacation—I figured out how to make or save the money, or we reduced our expectations. I gave away a little money to those clearly in greater need than I, and I chose to pay my own bills, which meant not asking for or accepting any alimony or child support even when my exhusband made much more than I did. My sons spent half of their time with their father, and I felt that since I was an able-bodied woman, all the financial responsibility for me and half the financial responsibility for the children I had decided to have was mine.

I am *not* advocating these choices as any kind of magical formula for increased prosperity. Neither are they in any way morally superior to other choices I could have made. These are simply the choices I made. We all have choices, although not always the same ones. Had I been a man or a woman of color, had I been better educated or wealthy or mentally or physically disabled, my resources and therefore my potential choices would have been different. The level of my income was a consequence of both my choices, based on what I valued, and the societal values of the time. I live in a culture where monetary profit is highly valued. This means that those whose talents generate high profits—baseball players and movie stars—are sometimes paid up to thousands of times more than those whose talents do not usually directly generate large monetary profits, such as teachers and writers and counselors.

Our responsibility is to work with the resources we have to do the best we can, taking care of the business at hand. And there is business to take care of. We and those who depend upon us need homes and clothing and food, we need that which takes care of our bodies, and we need that which feeds our minds and souls. That I would most often choose to spend the ten dollars I managed to hang on to from the weekly budget on a book or some cut flowers does not make these better choices than spending it on a movie or ruffled socks or taking a friend out for tea. When your spirit is tired and sagging, what lifts and encourages, what brings a smile to your face or lets your shoulders drop a little at the end of the day, can seem very strange to someone else. People are fed in different ways. We have choices not only in how we acquire the money we need but also in how we decide to spend it.

The more I took responsibility for my choices—both in making and spending money—the less poor I felt even though my income did not change. There was a time, when I was first divorced and living on my own, when any inquiries about my well-being would solicit information about my bank balance and budget. Afraid I would not be able to provide for myself and my sons and second-guessing the wisdom of my decision not to go out and get a "real" job, I defined how I was doing in terms of how much money I had—and I didn't have much, so how I was doing was poorly. Years later, living on exactly the same income, I realized I no longer felt poor. I simply felt blessed to be doing what I loved, to live in a time and a place where my children and I had a decent home and abundant opportunities to learn and create and participate in the world. Nothing had changed externally. What had changed was my sense of self and so, consequently, my relationship to money—the same amount of money. Where I had felt a victim, I had become a determiner by recognizing I had choices. When considering a purchase, I stopped saying, "I can't afford it," and started saying, "That's not where I want to spend that amount of money."

The less poor I felt, the more uncomfortable I was when I noticed myself using the mythology of poverty as a badge of worthiness to placate others. When someone would complain that they couldn't afford the fee for a retreat, I stopped justifying my fees by telling them how my sons and I lived well below the government-designated poverty line and simply expressed my genuine hope that their circumstances would change so they could participate in a retreat at a future date.

Once in a while someone would begin to argue that it was morally reprehensible to be accepting *any* fee for facilitating spiritual retreats or sharing spiritual teachings. It took me a few years to understand their objection. At the time I simply told them that so long as my housing co-op and grocery store would not take prayers in lieu of money for rent and food, I was going to be charging for my services.

It's not so much whether you should or should not sell spirituality, you simply can't. You cannot buy your spirituality from me or anyone else. I cannot sell you knowledge of your soul's deepest longing, an experience of your innately compassionate nature, or a connection to something larger than you because I don't have *your* knowledge, *your* experience, or *your* connection to sell. All I can do when I am facilitating retreats is provide you with a sacred container—a place and some practices that will give you the opportunity to do the work of opening to your own knowledge, experience, and connection—

and some stories that hopefully will inspire and encourage us all when we are lost or tired. I charge money for the time and energy it takes to do all of this so I can provide for myself and my family while I am doing it.

This may sound self-evident, but it is not so clear when you read some of the ads for spiritual workshops and seminars. Using a common business model, some promoters reduce spiritual experiences and knowledge to consumer products, listing what participants will get for their money: freedom from fear, an experience of the sacred, answers to life's problems, emotional balance, profound insight, self-knowledge, wisdom—all things that simply cannot be bought or sold.

If you are reading this chapter to find the formula for how you can multiply your income tenfold, I can save you some time. I don't know. And you should probably know I am not a big fan of the so-called prosperity consciousness workshops. With few exceptions, despite the rhetoric of benevolent and infinite abundance, I have found the two most common feelings these workshops cultivate and feed on are fear and greed. Being as susceptible to these as anyone, I try not to put myself in places that encourage the part of me that is tempted to define the quality of my life by the level of my bank balance—the part of me that is afraid. I want to take care of business in a way that is consistent with who I am, as a means to the end of living fully. I do not want to obsess about it as an end in itself.

Sometimes I do worry about money. The truth is that when I unconsciously fear that I am not enough—when I am not connected with my innately compassionate, gentle, and fully present nature—I sometimes find myself driven by the anxiety that there will not be enough. It is then that I behave in a stingy, grasping, and less-than-impeccable manner with regard to money.

It is 1997, and I am organizing a ceremonial retreat in the tradition of the intertribal council of shamans with whom I have trained. This particular retreat involves a demanding day-long dry fast and outdoor ceremonial dance, from dawn to dusk. I have already talked several potential participants out of registering by explaining the rigors involved. I want only participants who are familiar with and willing to meet the demands of traditional ceremony. Three places are left on the week-long retreat.

I have always prided myself on ensuring that financial concerns do not color my choices regarding the deeply personal and spiritual work I do with others. Or so I think. For some reason on this day I have a pang of worry that the retreat may not fill. Perhaps I'm anxious because the rigors of this ceremony combined with my own physical limitations mean I will not be able teach for several months afterward. Or maybe I doubt it will fill because the demands of this retreat eliminate a number of potential participants. Or maybe I'm just having a bad day and can feel worry nibbling at the edges of my finely honed budget as I consider the unexpected car repair or the fee for a recently announced school trip or the unanticipated rise in my monthly phone bill. Whatever the reason, I unconsciously experience a momentary crack in my resolve not to influence people's choices regarding these retreats and place a phone call to Fran, a woman who has expressed interest but not yet registered. Sometimes that's all it takes to get us into trouble—a moment of going unconscious about our motivation.

I get Fran's answering machine and leave a message. "Fran, Oriah here. Just checking in about your registration for the retreat. I do have three places left and would love to have you join us. I have turned several folks down, because I am really wanting to do this cer-

emony with people who know what they are getting into and are serious about what they are doing, people who can really do the dance in
a traditional manner. I think you would be one of those—so let me
know." I hang up. Nothing I have said is untrue, but I feel sick. I
know I have let my concern about the workshop filling—about making enough money—lead me to try to influence this woman's decision with flattery. I shake my head ruefully and sigh.

"Should have gone into advertising, Oriah. Nice bullshit!" I mut-
ter out loud, disgusted with myself. And as the words finish leaving
my mouth I hear the high beep of Fran's answering machine turning
off. I pause, frozen at my desk like a deer caught in the headlights of
an oncoming car. The speakerphone on my desk is turned on. My
words have been recorded by Fran's machine!

I panic. I turn the speakerphone off, but it's too late. What can I
do? I will be exposed as a completely underdeveloped spiritual
teacher motivated by her fear about money and willing to flatter a
student in order to get a registration. More important, I may have
negatively prejudiced this woman's decision and ruined her chance to
participate in a potentially life-transforming ceremony. I don't know
if karmic debt exists, but if it does, who knows what kind of karma
could be incurred for interfering with someone's spiritual journey?
And she'll tell others! She is a student of another teacher I greatly
admire. What will that teacher think when she hears of my manipula-
tive attempt to get Fran to register?

My elder son, Brendan, pops his head into my office and, seeing
my stricken look, asks what's wrong. I confess everything. He
struggles not to laugh and tries to reassure me.

I am inconsolable and get up to pace the small room. "I don't know
what happened. I just lost it for a minute. I never do that kind of

thing. And then I do it once—*once!*—and I get caught! Where's the justice in that?" I wail. "What am I going to do?"

"Nothing!" he says emphatically. "Don't do anything. You'll just make it worse." He goes downstairs. I can hear him telling his brother what I have done and the two of them laughing together in the living room.

I know I should just leave it alone, but I can't. What began as a momentary weakness now has me completely out of control. There must be a way to fix this. If God or the Universe or Anyone-in-Charge would just let me fix this, I promise I will never ever do anything like this again. I've learned my lesson. All thoughtful reflection has evaporated, and I am back in the let's-make-a-deal theology of my childhood.

A half hour later my sons come up to my office to see how I am. I am sitting at my desk staring woefully at the wall.

"Oh, no. You couldn't leave it alone, could you?" says Brendan without surprise. "What did you do?"

I confess that I have left a second message on Fran's machine concocting a ridiculously transparent lie, explaining that my comments after my original message had been directed at one of my sons coming into my office. "She won't buy it for a minute. I'm doomed."

Neither Brendan nor Nathan can stop laughing. There are few things more gratifying to teenagers than hearing one of their parents admit to the kind of stupidity of which they are regularly accused. "Have you learned nothing from watching sitcoms all these years?" Brendan shrieks. "One lie on top of another only leads to worse complications!"

And suddenly we are all laughing. He's right. It is like a TV sitcom. I have acted badly—twice! Driven first by a concern about money and then by a dread of being exposed as far less enlightened than I hope to appear, I have made a complete fool of myself. I laugh so hard tears come to my eyes. So much for being Ms. Impeccable in my financial dealings. So much for being the paragon of truth telling.

Fran calls later to register and tell me she didn't understand my second message. Apparently my muttered self-commentary did not register on her machine. I can see no point in further confusing her decision to participate with my neurosis so tell her it was nothing. I tell her to take her time deciding about the workshop, to be sure it is for her.

It helps to keep your sense of humor if you really want to see what you are doing and why. I have learned from this mistake: I am no longer so sure that I always impeccably separate finances from other teaching concerns; I have not, since this time, told anyone I thought they were suited for a workshop; and I make sure my speakerphone is off when talking to myself at my desk!

To take care of business without letting it determine who I am and how I treat both myself and others, I have to be aware of how I am feeling about myself and the world and my place in it. Part of taking care of the children—that includes me, those who depend upon me, and the world—is consciously deciding what the children really need. Does each of us really *need* our own bedroom, bathroom, phone, computer, car? Maybe. Maybe not. Beyond the meeting of basic survival needs there are thousands of choices to be made. And that's all they are—choices. I wanted personal control over my daily work schedule more than I wanted the security of a weekly paycheck and a benefit plan, so I chose to run my own business rather than work for someone else. I wanted financial independence and a life involved with the examination of spirituality more than I wanted the things a higher income could have bought me had I accepted child support or worked in another field. Choices. Just choices.

Over the years hundreds of men and women have told me their dreams—how they long to change their job or pursue their art, live in another country or leave their marriage but can't because they do not have the money. Knowing that business does have to be taken care of—the children do need to be fed—I would work with them to look at how they could live what they have declared is their soul's longing and still take care of business. I am a practical woman. And over the years I have realized that this valuable problem-solving process was not so much about finding a practical way to make dreams come true as about taking a necessary step to seeing that with very few exceptions it was never really about the money. It was about choices, choices influenced by personal preferences and sometimes dictated by fear.

Money is always a stand-in for something else, often a convenient stand-in. It beats having to haul my books around so I can exchange them for groceries or gasoline or movie tickets. And maybe because it always was intended to be a stand-in it is easy to let it stand in for whatever we fear we won't have enough of, don't deserve, or can never have. All you have to do is visit a divorce court and watch estranged husbands and wives give more than their combined incomes to lawyers in an effort to extract payment for all the loving, honoring, and cherishing withheld or refused. But the truth is, money is a poor replacement for the love or intimacy we want, for the spirituality or creativity we long to live more fully. And we know this. But each of us has our own fears about our worthiness, our own fear that we will not be enough. And so we reach and sacrifice and sometimes fight for the money and what we think it will buy—security, respect, power, freedom—and hope it will compensate for what we fear we are not.

What would you do if you knew you were enough just as you are today, if you knew—really *knew*—that you were in your essential nature a compassionate, gentle being capable of being fully present with yourself and the world? Would you trust yourself more? And how would that trust affect your choices about how to take care of business, how to get and spend your money?

### Meditation on Choices

Sit in a comfortable position with a pen and at least three sheets of paper nearby. Close your eyes, and bring your attention to your breath. Take three deep breaths in through your nose, and breathe out through your mouth, letting all the tension and tiredness in your body effortlessly flow away with your exhale. Feel your shoulders drop, and allow your mind to focus on your breath. Spend several minutes just watching your breath move in and out of your body. Be aware of the rising and falling of your body with the inhale and exhale. If thoughts come, acknowledge them and let them go, bringing your attention back to your breath.

Now pick up the pen and paper and begin to complete the statement "I love . . ." over and over. Make a list of all that comes to you now as that which you love. Be as specific as possible. The list may include people, places, things, feelings, activities—anything that comes to mind. When this process feels complete, close your eyes and focus once again on your breath, paying attention to the inhale and the exhale, the rising and falling of your body.

Now pick up the pen and a different sheet of paper and make a new list, completing the statement, "I value . . ." Write down all the things you value—the things you feel are important—in your life and the world. Be specific. Write down whatever comes to mind without judgment. Take your time. When this process feels complete, close your eyes and focus on your breath, taking three deep breaths in through your nose and breathing out through your mouth and letting your shoulders drop. Spend a few moments focusing your attention on your breath and letting all thoughts drift away.

Once again, pick up your pen and a third sheet of paper. This time finish the statements "I spend money on . . . ," "I spend time on . . . ," and "I spend energy on . . ." one after the other, then repeating all three over and over. Let your hand move on the page without analysis or judgment. What we seek is self-knowledge. Be honest about where your daily time, energy, and money are spent. No one else will see these lists unless you choose to share them. When you feel complete, for the final time, bring your attention to your breath and let your body relax. Let go with each exhale, and just sit following the breath in and out of your body for a few minutes.

Spread all three sheets of paper out in front of you, and reread what you have written. Do so without judgment, just seeing what is. See the relationship between the statements you have written. How much of your time, energy, and money is spent on things you love? How much is spent on things you value? How much is spent on things you neither love nor value? Why would you make a choice to spend any of your precious life—and time, money, and energy are manifestations of the life we have—on what you do not love or value? Could you make another choice? Do you want to? Perhaps you value things you did not realize you value. Or are these choices based on some-one else's values? Are any choices based on fear? With compassion, see the choices you are making and the consequences of these choices. Notice any feelings this information raises, and simply be with these feelings, without judgment.

# TEN

# *The Song*

~

*Show me how you offer to your people and the world
the stories and the songs you want our children's children to
    remember,
and I will show you how I struggle,
not to change the world, but to love it.*

When I was fifteen years old I wrote: *I want to live so that my life reflects the God I know.* How we live our lives is the story we choose to tell for our children's children to remember, reflects what we know of the Beloved, the Mystery, of that which is sacred. How you do what you do offers stories of hope or despair, of compassion or judgment, of presence or absence.

Michael and I are sharing a meal at a conference where we are both giving presentations. He speaks with deliberate precision, his words carefully chosen. Clearly he has said them before. "My vision," he tells me, "my work, is to change the world." I do not doubt his sincerity. Michael has dedicated his life to the work of creating personal and planetary change by working with spiritual groups, environmental causes, large corporations, and local communities. I would probably agree with most if not all of the changes he wants to create.

Why then, when he speaks so earnestly of changing the world, do I suddenly feel overwhelmed with a tired sadness? I do not speak, but I want to say, "I don't want to change the world anymore. I just want to learn how to love the world."

The world will change, is changing all the time, and I want to be a conscious part of that change. But I feel behind Michael's certainty and the words I might have once said myself a drivenness I suspect masks a terror in us both that we can never do enough or be enough. My throat closes with grief, and I feel an ache in the center of my chest.

I have spent long hours pondering my work in the world, trying to decide what to do with my life that will make the greatest contribution. And each time I go to the Grandmothers, the elders who have been my teachers for so many years, questioning if I should teach or write or speak or do something entirely different, their gentle but adamant response is always the same: "It doesn't matter, Oriah. It doesn't matter *what* you do. What matters is *how* you do whatever you choose to do."

I suppose if I were a fully enlightened being I would be able to do absolutely anything and be happy offering who I am to the world. I would be consistently compassionate and fully present whether I were making a meal or writing, washing the car or giving a talk, doing the laundry or studying. If I were a fully enlightened being I imagine I would be as content and openhearted planting trees or delivering mail or going to political rallies as I am writing or studying. I would be as present and compassionate waiting on customers at the corner store as I am facilitating a process of self-discovery for retreat participants. But I am not a fully enlightened being. I am a human being with likes and dislikes, gifts and talents, and challenges that change with time. My preferences do not make writing more important than tree planting or mail delivery or political rallies. Neither do they indicate that facilitating retreats contributes more to the world than waiting on customers at the corner store. If I were able to be more present and compassionate with store customers than I am with retreat participants, I would make a greater contribution to the world working in a store than leading another retreat. It is not what we do but how we do whatever we are doing that makes a difference. When we know ourselves we are able to make choices to do those things that, given our individual preferences and personalities, make it easier for us to be who we are—compassionate and openhearted and present. We are able to choose to do what we know we love.

This doesn't mean always doing what is easiest. There is a difference between happiness—offering who you are to the world and knowing it is enough—and pleasure or ease. At the moment I feel most able to offer who I am to the world when I am writing. But there are days when writing is neither easy nor pleasurable, when the words do not flow, when I think I would rather be cleaning the oven or giving the cat a bath. And if I found writing unpleasant and difficult most of the time, I would question if it was the best way for me to be spending this precious life. Still, pleasure and ease come and go, but I consistently find I am able to be more present and openhearted toward myself and the world when I write. So I write.

Each of us chooses the stories we will weave into the culture of our families and our communities and our world by how we do whatever we do. How we do what we do reflects the song we hear inside—what we believe to be true about our essential selves—and this is the song we teach our children, regardless of what we tell them.

In both my writing and my speaking I tell stories. I choose the stories that remind me of who we really are, of how our essential nature makes us capable of great compassion, courage, and wisdom. But sometimes—often—a story chooses me. Sometimes it's a story I have dismissed as too small and ordinary to share, a story I fear might be judged as lightweight or not spiritually meaningful, a story that simply refuses to go away and give ground on the page to stories of great teachers and leaders. And finally I surrender to the story that wants to be told, and in telling the story I listen for the song it sings, the dance it teaches me. In the medicine teachings of the elders with whom I have trained, love is the catalyst energy—that which transforms us. And so, of course, it is a love story.

At forty-five I had reached a point in my life when the ache for a mate was a comfortable longing I could revisit. I was no longer sure what I had been looking for from relationships over the years, but I suddenly had faith that I would recognize it if and when I saw it. I had been celibate by choice—although not always contentedly—for almost five years.

And then, one day a letter arrived. The writing on the envelope looked familiar. Inside the note said, "I was staring outside my window at work, wondering how you were. I put your name into my Internet search engine and found this address. Has it really been thirty years?" At the bottom of the letter was a name I had not thought of in years.

In 1970, when I was fifteen years old, I went on a church-organized canoe trip for teenagers in Algonquin Park. For two weeks I spent most of my time paddling a canoe and talking endlessly with Jeff, a bright, gawky seventeen-year-old who built telescopes, took photographs, composed beautiful piano music, and wrote poetry. And for the first time in my life, I fell in love. Like most fifteen-year-old girls, I felt like I had been waiting for love forever. I expected it to be like it was in the movies—being swept off your feet by someone who was more godlike than any seventeen-year-old boy could ever hope to be. Instead, it was finding yourself walking beside your best friend. It was like suddenly being connected to someone lung to lung, finding yourself barely about to breathe without the contact.

Jeff's family lived in Niagara Falls, four hundred miles south of my home in northern Ontario. After the canoe trip we wrote dozens of long letters to each other and saw each other three or four times over the next two years when my family went south to visit my grandparents or when I could convince my parents that attending a church youth retreat in southern Ontario was critical for my spiritual development.

But in all that time he never kissed me. I know it may seem silly to say now, but it broke my heart. And the first time your heart is broken—just like every other time to come—the pain sears through you.

I remember one night in particular. I was attending a conference in Niagara Falls, and the two of us went out for a walk. The evening air was crisp and cold, the dark sky gleaming with stars and every branch of every tree brushed with a fine layer of snow that sparkled from the lights around the park. We walked through the snow, and when he reached for my hand I thought, "This is it. We are here alone, it's a beautiful night. If he doesn't kiss me tonight it's simply because he does not find me attractive."

Do you remember when anticipating a kiss made your stomach tighten into a hard knot and your insides quiver like you had hypothermia? I couldn't stop shaking. I felt that there was a good chance I might pass out. Over just a kiss! I was equally afraid that the kiss would happen and that it wouldn't, worried that I might have bad breath or just be a very bad kisser.

It never occurred to me that Jeff might be equally nervous. I don't know if it's changed, but in those days fifteen-year-old girls knew little or nothing about what was going on inside seventeen-year-old boys. They were the ones in charge, the ones who were supposed to take the initiative. Now, having been privy to small bits of the anguish and uncertainty felt by my two teenage sons, I know better. But thirty years ago I was sure that if Jeff felt any of what I felt, if the endless conversations and long letters had meant to him a fraction of what they had to me, he would simply kiss me.

So when he moved away from me without touching me, I just stood there in the middle of the park and felt my heart drop down inside my body and break like a small raw egg somewhere in the bottom of my boots. I started to cry and walked back to the conference center alone.

After that the letters between us got more and more infrequent. It sounds like such a little thing: the disappointment of not being kissed, of believing I had been mistaken about the feeling between us. Everyone has their first love, their first heartbreak. It's part of life. But I wonder if we too easily disregard the effect these early woundings have on our hearts. As author Anne Lamott says, there is only one way to move through grief, and that is by grieving. But at fifteen I had no idea how to do that. I just wanted to diminish the pain as quickly as possible and to protect myself from similar heartache in the future. So for months after I walked away from Jeff in that park I would give myself a lecture each night before falling asleep, ruthlessly telling myself I had to simply face facts: people were not going to be drawn to me and that was just the way it was; I simply was not attractive and would have to find other ways to win over those with whom I wanted to be close; I'd have to work at it.

And then began years of believing I had to earn love, of guarding myself against receiving what was freely offered. How easy it was to believe there was something inherently and basically wrong with me.

When I read Jeff's unexpected note thirty years later, none of this came to mind. I was just delighted to hear from an old friend and wanted to give him a call to catch up on our lives. We swapped vital statistics: he had been married and was now divorced; he still had hair on his head and was no longer skinny; he still composed music, took photographs, played the piano, wrote poetry, and built telescopes. As a printed circuit board designer, he had fulfilled one of the dreams he had talked about as a teenager to have something of his own design up in space. I promised to send him a copy of the book I had written, and we agreed to get together for dinner sometime in the near future.

The next day I couriered Jeff a copy of the book and waited. Sometime earlier a disgruntled exlover had sent me a letter after reading *The Invitation*, rather snidely calling it "the longest personal ad" he had ever read. I'd laughed out loud. I wasn't offended, although I did think that he had chosen to miss a great deal of what the book was about. Still, while the book was about much more than just the longing for intimate relationship, it certainly included a sense of both the depth of my desire and the intensity of my struggle in this area of my life.

A day later I received an e-mail from Jeff. He had read the book in one sitting and wrote,

> I opened the book and read your inscription and my eyes sort of glazed over. It has been almost thirty years, and here was the same

handwriting, the same tone of voice, and the same clear thought that had made my heart soar before I even knew what to do about it. . . . Despite that long road that has taken you to your present ability to bare your soul . . . the passion for sharing your feelings and really finding out about what makes others tick was virtually the same as back on the shores of Opeongo. . . . I AM SO PROUD OF YOU. . . . And although I often thought years ago that somehow I had failed myself by letting the love of my life slip through my grasp, reading your book revalidated my feelings for you and my love for myself. I wasn't wrong about you or myself, and there was nothing to grasp, only something to hold deep inside and treasure.

I was a goner. I kept reading *I AM SO PROUD OF YOU*. He was the only person who could really know that the woman who had written *The Invitation* was in fact the same person as the passionate and outspoken girl who had laughed and paddled and talked her way through Algonquin Park thirty years earlier. He had seen me, and this seeing, this loving, gave him the right to be proud, pleased for my success and happy that I had stayed in some essential way true to who I was. And being seen in this way opened my heart to myself and the possibilities of love once again.

We arranged to have dinner at my home two weeks later and continued to e-mail, sometimes several times a day. Years ago our relationship had flourished through letters, so it seemed natural to reestablish our communication through the written word. We covered it all: our sexual and emotional histories; our views on money, marriage, spirituality, work, and children; our memories of what had and hadn't happened between us thirty years earlier and why. He felt he had blown it. Madly in love and unable to believe that I would return his affection and believing, as most boys then did, that "good" girls were not interested in physical affection (let alone sex!), he'd felt paralyzed, unable to risk offending or losing me by moving toward me.

Feeling my heart racing ahead of what my head thought wise, I wrote all kinds of warnings: I was not going to have more children; I was not sure I could ever live with anyone again; my health was often not strong and I had to pace my level of activity; I did not want to be the central or sole focus of any man's life; neither would I make any man this kind of focus in mine.

It's a wonder the man showed up for dinner.

But he did. And none too soon. I'd been a nervous wreck all week. My writing had grown incoherent until I had finally given up trying to produce a decent sentence on the page. I'd hardly eaten anything for days. What if the connection through the e-mails simply evaporated when we saw each other in person? Worse, what if it evaporated for one of us and not the other? What if it didn't evaporate but was even stronger in person?

When the day of the dinner finally arrived I was no less nervous than I had been thirty years earlier waiting for him to kiss me in the park. I kept telling myself to calm down, reminding myself that I was forty-five, not fifteen, and if I didn't stop it I was going to make myself sick. It didn't help. When I heard the doorbell I honestly thought I might pass out from lack of oxygen. My body seemed incapable of comprehending my brain's command to "Breathe!"

And there he was, grinning at the door. And all my nervousness just fell away. He came in, put down the flowers he had brought, put his arms around me, and kissed me. Pulling back, looking at me, and laughing he said, "There! That was probably the most important kiss of my life, and it only took me thirty years to get to it!"

That first night when he came for dinner he was fearless. He told me, "It was always you, Oriah. If a genie had popped out of a bottle and said, 'You can spend the rest of your life with any woman on the planet,' it always would have been you."

This, of course, terrified me. For the next few months we had a wonderful time together punctuated by my panic, my fear that after all I had said I wanted I just couldn't do it—I couldn't be in intimate relationship and do my work, take care of my health and my sons, and still find time for myself. Despite the wonderful time we had together, I could work myself into a lather between visits thinking about how different our lives were, how little we had in common. I snarled about going to see his family—and then had a lovely time. We arranged to rent a cottage together for three weeks in the summer, and then I told him that if we didn't last that long I could always buy him out of his half or we could split the time. I told him I loved him and then kept one hand on the doorknob just in case.

And through it all he just simply refused to stop loving me. He told me once, during one of my what-was-I-thinking, I-can't-do-this panics, "Oriah, if you really ever feel that it is bad for you to be with me, then I will go. I think being together can make your life and your work easier, but maybe I'm wrong. But what I do know is this: you will never find a man who will love you more than I do."

And I believe him. But I have been alone for a very long time. It is a paradox of middle age that the experience we have accumulated makes emotional risk taking both easier and harder. Easier because you know you will survive the disappointments; harder for the same reason. You know you will survive even if the hurt feels like it will kill you. You will survive with one more scar, one more dark stain of grief on your heart, and you're not sure you want to risk living with one more place on your body and soul that will ache when the rains come, reminding you of what was once hoped for or promised

I have moments when I look at Jeff and think of our story—the deep connection at such a young age, the thirty years of separation, and the unexpected reunion—and I throw up my hands and wonder why I spend one minute planning and worrying and trying to choreograph my life, trying to protect myself from the risks involved in loving and being loved. Surely something larger than myself is at work here. And I know that does not mean for one second that I am not responsible for the choices I make.

From the night of that first dinner we have spent every available weekend together. Jeff lives in a small city an hour and a half from my home. We've relived the past and found ourselves in a present together still learning who the other is—and always was. He tells me a story of how at eighteen, determined to win me back, he built a mass spectrometer, a machine that separates heavy atoms from light atoms.

I look at him, baffled. "You built a mass spectrometer to win me back?"

"Well . . . yeah," he admits, looking more seventeen than forty-seven. "I thought that if I won the science fair award and had my picture in the paper you would be impressed and figure I was worth waiting for."

I am flabbergasted. "You were going to win the girl back by building a mass spectrometer?" Laughing, I throw my arms around him. "That is the sweetest and the geekiest thing I have ever heard." We are both laughing. "Wouldn't flowers have been easier? It didn't surprise me that you won the science fair award. But I already knew you were smart, you fool! I just wanted you to kiss me!"

So he did.

I don't know what will happen with Jeff and me. I have to stay in the present. But I am finding myself trusting this love that has brought us back together a little more each day. I no longer panic when I feel us out of sync—when I am at a silent Buddhist retreat meditating and writing and he is at the pub with friends watching the hockey playoffs and having a couple of beers. I either wait until the normal ebb and flow brings us back into closer contact or reach across and touch him with the truth of whatever I am feeling. That's the biggest thing I am learning—that the fastest way to reconnect is to tell the truth, however awkwardly, however terrifying. When I tell him I am afraid, he is just with me in the fear, and it grows smaller, and together we figure out what each of us needs and what we need together, and then I find myself able to write or able to say I need Friday night to myself without fearing that he will move away or move in closer than I can bear at the moment.

On one occasion, having told him once again of my reservations and my lofty hopes and dreams for relationship, I said, as if confiding a well-kept secret, "You know, there are easier women to love, women who are not so driven, women who are not always trying to do everything right, trying to be conscious. . . ."

He just laughed and said, "Oh, Oriah, I already know that! Remember—I met your mother and your grandmother. You come from a long line of women who are not 'easy.' I don't want easier. I want you."

I considered being offended on behalf of the women of my family, but it's hard to muster self-righteous indignation about the truth when it's so lovingly offered. And it's a relief to be so known, to be with someone who knows that the blue-gray of my eyes—the same blue-gray of the eyes of my mother and her mother before her—reflects not only a lineage of bright minds and soft-edged sorrows but also the cool steel of relentlessly strong wills.

On that first night of our reunion Jeff brought me the sixty letters I had written him so many years ago. He told me, "I want these back, but I thought you might like to take a look at them, to see that what I said is true, that everything you are writing about now was right there thirty years ago."

And it was. In page after page of blue fountain pen ink on pale pink paper that still held the faint scent of a girl's perfume, I read of my constant questions about God and life and who I am. I read of my deep desire to make a difference in the world and my worries about doing well enough, being enough. And all of this is mixed in with reports on the weather and the church choir, complaints about my parents, and admonishments to Jeff not to give up his piano lessons.

The letters make me wonder if we ever really change. And I think again of the Grandmother's words from the dream and realize the task is not to change, the task is simply to become all of who we are. The letters I wrote when I was fifteen reflect who I am and always have been, but the girl who wrote those letters was still largely unknown to herself. The soul's joy is in unfolding, in becoming known to the self and being able to live from a deeper and deeper connection with who we really are. While this is an introspective task we have to do for ourselves, there can be no doubt that being seen and known and loved by another offers us the warm light of encouragement that softens our hearts to ourselves when we are discouraged about our human failings.

Once, shortly after we got back together, Jeff said to me, "I was with other women who made me content, but they never made me dream. You make me dream."

To dream is to create the stories of how we live our lives, and these are the stories our children's children will remember. I write with as much honesty and frankness as I can, because I want to offer stories of being present with what is. I recite poetry when I speak, because I want to offer beauty and the power of art to remind us of who and what we are. I share personal stories, because I want to cocreate a story of intimacy and cultivate our capacity for compassion in dealing with our human failings. I tell love stories because I want to learn how to love well.

### *Meditation on the Stories Our Lives Are Telling*

Sometimes I focus my meditation on questions that help me see the choices I am making and the dreams of my heart. You may want to write after each of the questions suggested here, or you may just want to sit with each question, asking it repeatedly and seeing what comes.

Sit in a comfortable position. If you are planning on writing, make sure a pen and paper are nearby. Close you eyes, and take three big breaths in though your nose, breathing out through your mouth. Let your shoulders drop on the exhale, and allow your weight to drop down to the bottom of your body, feeling the surface beneath you and the earth farther below supporting you. Bring your attention to your breath. Just follow the inhale and the exhale, watching your body rise and fall, breathing normally. If thoughts come, acknowledge them and let them float away easily with the out-breath, like clouds drifting across a clear blue sky, bringing your attention back to your breath. Spend a few minutes just following your breath as it moves in and out of your body.

Now, staying in this quiet and relaxed state, allow the questions to come and sit with them: What if it really doesn't matter what you do? What if all that really matters is how you do whatever you do? What would you do? How would you do it? Just sit with these questions, and follow your breath. Let whatever thoughts or feelings come, and sit with them. You may want to write some of them down, or you may choose to simply be with them as they come, focusing again and again on your breath and repeating the questions to yourself.

Now bring your attention back to your breath. Let all

thoughts go with the exhale, and simply focus on the rising and the falling of your body with the breath. Take a few moments and be with your breath. Then, let the question come: What would I do if it weren't so risky? Again, you may want to write down your responses to the question, or you may want to simply sit with the thoughts and feelings that come as you repeat the question to yourself.

When you feel complete, come back once again to your breath, bringing your attention to the inhale and the exhale and letting all thoughts go. Spend a couple of moments focused on your breath. Breathe into any places in your body where there may be stress or tension, and let it harmlessly melt away with the exhale. Then, allow yourself to focus on the questions: How do you make love to the world? If the way you are with yourself with those you love and know and those who are strangers tells a story, what kind of story is your life telling the world?

Allow whatever comes to come. Whatever the response—thoughts, feelings, more questions—be with it. Breathe with it, and repeat the questions to yourself. How do you make love to the world? What is the story your life is telling?

# ELEVEN

# The Dance of Shared Solitudes

*Sit beside me in long moments of shared solitude,*
*knowing both our absolute aloneness and our undeniable belonging.*
*Dance with me in the silence and in the sound of small daily words,*
*holding neither against me at the end of the day.*

I ache for shared silence, not the awkward lulls in conversation where we reach for something, anything, to cover the tension of trying to be with too much of the other and too little of ourselves, but the moments of fullness that let each of us unfold and know who we really are. I long for silences with another where there is nothing to forgive or explain or justify, where we agree to abandon quickly spoken words for a time so we do not abandon ourselves or each other, the silences where no one asks me to choose between belonging to myself and being with the world. And when these silences come, I feel how I am working my way home through whatever they hold—terror or tenderness, grief or celebration—spiraling ever closer to a sweetness I have ached for all my life.

Natalie, the beautiful nine-year-old daughter of my friend Valerie, is dead. Cancer. Three hundred of us sit in the church, and Natalie stares back at us unafraid from the photo at the front. Everyone wears dark suits or polite dresses and cries quietly or stares stoically ahead as the minister speaks about life continuing. I love words, but I do not want words now. I want silence and keening and the sound of tearing cloth. I pray that the words are offering something to ease the incomprehensible ache that must be in the hearts of Natalie's mother and father and sisters, but I long to be silent together. I stare at my hands clenched in my lap and struggle to find a way to breathe and be with these people—my people. We are neither alone enough with the grief that is tearing each of us apart—grief for all the children and all the innocence we have lost—nor with each other enough in that grief to risk shared silence. If we could risk such intimacy, surely the collective wail that could carry us across to the other side of this ache would find us and fill us.

But we don't know how.

I think of my own sons when they were small: of carrying Brendan on one hip, keeping a hand free to pick up clothes and toys as I walked through the house talking to him, and suddenly as I turned away from the window I saw our shadowed silhouette on the bedroom wall— mother and child as one whole; of Nathan crawling into my lap whenever I sat down, fitting snugly there and claiming my attention and my heart with his small warm body no matter how tired or distracted I was. I think of how, when they were young, afraid I would forget who I was, I turned for a moment to speak to the world so I could hear the sound of my own voice and know I had not disappeared, and when I turned back to my babies they were young men walking out the door of their mother's house into the world, as all young men must.

This coming together and moving apart is what makes us aware that we are all, each of us, alone. And when I am fully with myself, it is almost enough. Almost. But when you hold my aloneness and I hold yours, when I know we will not hold the necessary silences against each other, I am penetrated by a greater intimacy, an intimacy with the Other, the Mystery that permeates everything, that penetrates and vibrates in my skin, your blood, my bones. It is what makes my breath and your breath the same breath, breathing us all into the next moment. It is here, where my solitude and yours sit side by side, that I know this Other that is never completely other, that I meet the *I* that is not simply myself, that I am truly with the world.

This is how I want to dance together, over and over again, so that even when we are apart you are both with me and without me as you were when we sat next to each other. This—this solitude and merging with each other that lets us remember the Great Silence that sustains us—is the home my soul seeks.

I have to go there alone.

I cannot go there without you.

This is the experience of deep contemplation, and even when it is done in physical isolation—in solo time at a hermitage or on a wilderness vision quest—it does not remove us from others but opens us to a deeper intimacy with both ourselves and world. When we are profoundly *with* ourselves we find ourselves *with* the world.

But we do not live in a culture that teaches or values the contemplative aspect of life. What reflection occurs is pigeonholed into mutually exclusive categories. Academics examine the individual and the world with supposedly detached rationality, dismissing stories of the heart as anecdotal. Therapists and the personal growth community focus on individual histories, often shying away from seeing them in the larger context of the history of the culture, the planet, or the cosmos. Those interested in spirituality, reacting against the overvaluing of the empirically provable and the domi-nance of linear thinking, often focus exclusively on the intuitive and experiential, refusing to use their thinking to examine the mystical explanations being offered for experiences that seem to defy scien-tific explanation.

To dance, to be all of who and what we are, we cannot leave any part of the self behind. It is not enough to have an experience of the unity or the solitude and refuse to use our thinking—intuitive, cre-ative, and rational—to explore possible explanations for such experi-ences. It is not enough to analyze and dissect with the rational mind and leave behind what the heart knows because the mind cannot find a niche for this knowledge in some neat, well-developed schema. It is not enough to romanticize and make infallible the impulses of the body or emotions, insisting something must be good and true because I feel it.

Some spiritual traditions and New Age philosophies claim that our true nature is to be found exclusively in the experience of our unity with all life. They deny the reality of our separation, claiming that it is only an illusion of time and space. But I live here, in time and space. This is the reality I know every day, and in this reality no two mate-rial beings can occupy the same space at the same time. We are sepa-rate. Why is this any less real than those experiences of merging with another or feeling myself a part of a vast wholeness? Conversely, some in the scientific community advocate a materialist philosophy that denies the reality of any experience of merging with something greater than the self, reducing such experiences to the biochemical processes of the brain or the delusional meandering of a wishful imagination. To dance, to step into the fray of daily life and to keep true to our soul's intention to live who we really are, we have to be willing to live both the reality of our separate individuality and the reality of our unity in something greater.

Each day at 7 A.M. the seventeen men and women attending the writing retreat assemble in a room where the windows look out over the river. I share some poetry and a prayer and lead them in a meditation. The meditation is done in pairs, sitting close, facing each other. Each person in turn uses their imagination to visualize a blessing for the person opposite them coming up from the earth and flowing into their own hands. Slowly they reach out and touch the head of the man or woman in front of them, imagining this blessing flowing into the person, letting their fingers touch the shape and the softness of the face before them, seeing the incredible beauty of the other. As each person receives, they open themselves to beginning their day blessed. Finishing the meditation, we wander out onto the land. We watch the great blue heron fly down the river, catch a glimpse of the otter's head skimming through the water, stand beneath the maple tree listening to the river begin its rush through the gorge until the dining room bell calls us to breakfast.

The agreement we have is to be in social silence from the time we get up until our first session at 10 A.M. Each person fills a plate with food and moves to the tables in the log cabin dining room or on the porch outside. The first morning you can catch the scent of tension in those who are not used to this, those who are unsure what will be expected of them if they are not speaking or listening to others. But by the second day this anxiety has been dispelled. Nothing is expected. All that is asked is that each person hold the silence. The meal—the morning itself—slows down. In the silence it is easier to be aware of each mouthful, every taste, the movement of hand to mouth, the sound of metal cutlery laid on a china plate.

By the fourth morning there is a rhythm to our hours of silence together, an easy dance of people moving through the room, shifting chairs, no longer avoiding sitting too close or too far away but letting the impulse to move take them to a spot that draws them.

On the last morning of the retreat I am sitting on the porch overlooking the property eating my ginger pancakes slowly, surrounded by five other women at various tables: Vivian in her blue flannel teddy bear pajamas cradles a mug of warm tea in her hands; Suzy eats fruit and muffins slowly, gazing outward like a woman trying to catch a glimpse of her husband returning from the sea; Ellen, quiet with her thoughts, turned inward and breathing, just breathing; Myrna, the eldest in our group, now approaching the threshold of sixty, her red hair blazing like fire as the sun climbs higher, her long legs gracefully stretched out, painted toes relaxed and glittering in delicate black sandals. Cat, the youngest, sits behind Myrna curled up in her chair, writing in a journal and crying quietly. Suddenly a great sob escapes her, shaking her—shaking us all for a moment. No one moves. No one speaks. We are with her as we are with each other, and yet each of us is at the same time completely alone with all the unspent sobs we hold inside.

Cat's sob and the tenderness of the morning blessing and the silence we are holding together split me open. A trickle of fear ripples though me like a small electrical shock, but it vanishes almost as quickly as it appears. There is no pain, only an almost unbearable and exquisite sensation of being fully alive. For one moment I am alone enough—no one to take care of, no one asking for explanations or time or movement—and I am at the same time enough with the world, with these five women and this place and this moment. The wind shakes the leaves on the quaking aspen before me, and I feel the flutter of their sound in my chest. I hear, as if for the first time, the wail of trucks on the highway in the distance carrying lives away from me, and I know I am as connected to those whose names I will never learn as I am to those who share this porch with me. The rising heat of the morning sets the cicadas buzzing and warms the great pine on the front lawn, sending its sweet scent to fill me. And I feel how the heat of the sun and the heat of my body are the same heat and yet separate, distinct.

The German theologian Meister Eckhart wrote: *There is nothing in all the universe so much like God as silence*. Remembering that morning at the retreat and smiling at my own audacity, I think, "Close. But I would say, 'There is nothing in all the universe so much like God as *shared* silence.'"

Because it is where I am simultaneously aware of both my solitude and my deep connection with others that the experience of the sacred enters. Silence invites me into my solitude, makes me aware of my distinct and separate existence. To be aware of who and what I am, there must be a boundaried *I* as both subject and object. I must be conscious that there is a place where I end, there on the surface of my skin, at the top of my head and the tips of my fingers and toes, and a place where the other—the air around me, the chair beneath me, the hand touching mine—begins. It is this awareness of separation that gives me the gift of self-reflectivity. I am not only the *I* that perceives and experiences her separate existence, I am the *I* that is aware of the *I* that perceives and experiences this separation from the other. This apperception gives me the gift of exploring and knowing my own essential nature.

When the silence is held and shared with others, I taste this essential nature, my innate ability to be fully with another—compassion.

It is our compassionate nature that makes the boundary where I end and the other begins porous, that gives me the ability to experience the other as another myself despite the fact that we are separate and distinct individuals. In shared silence, where I am simultaneously aware of both my solitude and my deep connection with others, my awareness is opened to both my own essential nature and to the knowledge that this nature is the same as that which is embodied in all else—that which is greater than the sum of the parts, the Mystery. And I become aware of my participation in this wholeness.

Experiencing both my solitude and my unity with all that is, I know two things that have always been true: I belong in a profound and irrevocable way to those around me, to the world and to that which is greater than myself; and I am worthy of this belonging because I am an embodiment of the sacred presence that creates all that is. And this knowledge of my inherent belonging offers me the only freedom there is—freedom from fear.

Years ago at a gathering in a small Irish cottage, I heard the gifted philosopher and writer John O'Donohue speak. Standing in front of the hearth where a small peat fire burned, John stood gazing out at the mist-soaked moors. And then gently, in a voice full of that Irish lilt that makes all words sing with their innate poetry, he said, "Here's the truth of it." My heart started to beat more rapidly the way your heart does when you know you are about to hear something upon which your life depends. John smiled a little and continued with a conviction that mirrored my own sudden certainty that what he was saying was something I had always known. "The truth is that you *belong* here, and truly, not a hair on your head can be harmed."

His words articulated the knowledge I have experienced in the deep contemplation of shared silence: the certainty that while my heart may ache, my body may be injured, and my mind be distressed, truly no harm can ever come to my essential nature because it is made of the stuff of which everything is made. And so there is simply nothing to fear. And in the moments when we remember what we are and so are fearless, we are able to effortlessly make the choices that are consistent with our deepest soul's longing.

Moments of shared silence and of deep contemplation can be hard to find in the midst of our busy, chaotic, and sometimes noisy lives. Often I find myself enmeshed in thoughts or actions that are far from compassionate. Sometimes the separation between me and others—particularly those I love—feels like an impenetrable barrier. And nowhere is this more true than in those intimate relationships where the dizzying fullness of falling in love seems at moments only to highlight the ways in which we are separated from and incomprehensible to each other.

Jeff is sitting at the other end of the dining room table. We have returned from the theater to share dinner in my home with my sons and two close friends. Jeff has changed into more comfortable clothes—a pair of jeans and a T-shirt under a long-sleeved cotton shirt. The shirt hangs open because it is missing three buttons. A brown two-day-old coffee stain runs down one side of the shirt beside threads that hang where buttons were once fastened. And now, as I gaze at him across the table, I notice another food stain, larger and less identifiable, near the bottom of the underlying T-shirt. It's a college T-shirt. He has not been in college for over twenty-five years. And just above this stain is a fist-sized tear that exposes the pale pink flesh of his ample belly. He notices my scrutiny and looks at me inquiringly. He has not shaved today and is a month overdue for a haircut.

And I do not think to myself, "Here is the man I love, someone who is in his essential nature, like me, a gentle and compassionate person, capable of being fully present with himself and the world," even though I know this to be true. No. I think to myself, "Oriah, you can't end a relationship with someone you love because of the way he dresses." And I am not so sure that this is true.

We talk about it later, in between sharp-edged words about the unwashed pots and pans, the sarcastic comment I made last Sunday, and whether or not our physical appearance does or should affect the way we feel about each other. Most of our small daily words are more neutral: I can pick up the dry cleaning if you get dinner started. Have you seen my glasses? What time is the parent-teacher interview? This is the stuff of daily life. But whether the words and feelings that pass between us are benign or accusing, whether the silences are strained distances or simply busy preoccupation, real intimacy depends on our ability to regularly experience our own essential nature—that nature that allows us to experience our connection with the other. Real intimacy depends on our ability to find those silences that are shared openings.

Strangely, it is sometimes easier to find these shared silences with fellow retreat participants we hardly know or with strangers on a bus or in a theater than it is with the people we know well. But even there, where we have fewer hopes or fantasies or expectations of others, it is not easy. Speaking about the pleasure of those mornings of shared silence at the writing retreat, one of the participants, Christina, commented at the end of the week, "The reason people don't do this is not because they want to connect with each other by talking. Being silent together connects us in a much deeper way than morning chitchat. People don't do this because it's too intimate, too scary."

I know she is right and I wonder why. Why would we fear and avoid the very thing for which we long? Are we afraid that the other or we ourselves will not meet expectations? More the latter than the former, I think. I have seen it again and again in the eyes of those who are about to go out into the wilderness to pray and fast alone for the first time, the fear that even with no other person in the immediate vicinity they will be revealed by such intimate solitude as more shallow or bad tempered, less serious or sincere or capable—in some essential way less worthy—than any other man or woman who has ever dared to send out a prayer. We are afraid that what we bring to real intimacy—our selves—will not be enough.

Ironically, afraid that deep intimacy with ourselves or others will reveal some lack in our basic character, we avoid the very practices that would allow us to experience our essentially sacred and compassionate being. Afraid of this intimacy, we hang on to those things that create distance and distract us from being together. We hold against ourselves and each other the strained silences, the relentlessness of small daily words that deal with the seemingly infinite logistics of a human life, the torn T-shirts and unwashed dishes, the unkind words and messy bathrooms. And the chasm between who we are and who we know ourselves to be widens, the abyss between us and the man or the woman we once thought we could not live without deepens. And we think it is us, but we hope it is them that's the problem.

I will tell you my all-time favorite intimate bedroom fantasy. It is of a lying in bed next to the man I love, each of us reading a book. Really—that's it. Oh, our legs—the ones that are next to each other—may be touching or even intertwined, and we might pause now and then to read a particularly good piece of writing to each other, but each of us is engrossed in reading a different book. You could say that the nature of this fantasy just shows that I'm getting older, and you might be right. I know I'm getting older because lately the details of this fantasy, which have always included a beautiful bed with a warm duvet set in front of a fireplace, now include a pair of bright reading lamps and two pairs of eyeglasses. But the essence of the image—of being with another, deeply and intimately connected and yet still with myself—remains the same. I want, as the German poet Rainer Maria Rilke wrote, the marriage that happens when two people become the "guardians of each other's solitude."

This is what it is to live the beauty of a human life: to know my separateness, the place where I end and the rest of the world begins, to experience it next to another and be opened to my belonging, my undeniable participation in and embodiment of the compassionate Mystery that creates and sustains us all.

### *Meditation on the Truth of Who You Are*

On the last day of a writing retreat I led a meditation asking each person to sit in silence and then write the truest statement possible about themselves. I sat for a moment, expecting to write and rewrite statements that would take me deeper and deeper into the essence of the truth about myself. But instead, after only a minute or two, I picked up my pen and wrote, "I am blessed." I knew immediately that it was the truest statement I could write about myself. Of course, when I do this meditation at other times, other insights into myself have come, although it always remains true that I am indeed blessed.

Sit comfortably with a pen and paper nearby. Close your eyes and take three deep breaths in through your nose, exhaling through your mouth. Let the muscles of your back relax with each exhale, feeling your shoulders drop and your weight settle into the bottom of your body. With each exhale, let go of all the tiredness and tension in your body. Spend a few minutes just focusing your attention on your breath, following the exhale and the inhale, the rising and falling of your body. If thoughts come, simply acknowledge them and let them go, bringing your attention back to your breath.

Now ask yourself, "What is the truest statement I could write about myself right now?" When you are ready, without judgment, pick up your paper and pen and write the statement that comes. Then, just sit with it. What feelings does it elicit? What thoughts? Be with any thoughts or feelings that come without getting caught in them—just watching them come and go. Ask yourself if there is a statement you could write that would be truer than the one you have written. If so, what is it?

Write it. If not, simply stay with the statement you have written. Repeat this process with any new statements that come, simply sitting with the truth you know about yourself in this moment, without judgment. Bring your attention back to your breath, and sit with the statements that come and any feelings they raise.

# TWELVE

# The Sacred Emptiness

~~

*And when the sound of all the declarations of our sincerest*
*intentions has died away on the wind,*
*dance with me in the infinite pause before the next inhale*
*of the breath that is breathing us all into being,*
*not filling the emptiness from the outside or from within.*

Sometimes I think there are only two instructions we need to follow to develop and deepen our spiritual life: slow down and let go. Doing both is necessary if we want to live with the sacred emptiness at the center of our being, that which can renew us and remind us to simply be all of who we are.

Shirley's voice sounds very young to me on the phone. She is twenty-six. Three years ago, while she was a university student, Shirley was in a car accident that left her quadriplegic—able to breathe on her own, all her mental faculties intact, but without feeling or movement from the neck down. After the injury Shirley returned home to be taken care of by her mother, but a subsequent car accident a year later left her mother disabled. Shirley now lives in a rehabilitation hospital and visits her family on the weekends. I have agreed, at her father's request, to spend some time with her if that is what Shirley wants.

We chat for a while, and then I ask Shirley what she is hoping to receive from any time we might spend together. I don't want to mislead her about what I can offer. She has had enough disappointment in her young life.

"I know my dad is worried about me, but I think I am doing pretty well. I just want to know why this has happened to us—my accident and my mother's. Some people say that when things like this happen there's something you're supposed to learn. I'm hoping you can tell me what that is."

I tell her the truth. "I can't even imagine what it has been like for you and your family. I've had some hard things happen in my life, so I understand why you want to find a reason for it all." I pause and slow down. "I just don't think we can know why things like this happen. I think our task—and this is sometimes very difficult—is to live with all that is hard in our lives without being able to know why it happens and still find a way to fully choose life, every day."

I pause. How does a twenty-six-year-old who cannot move find a way to live fully? I don't know the range of what she has loved and lost. Was she an athlete? Did she have a lover? Did she enjoy walking, hiking, dancing, cooking? Did she revel in touching and being touched, feeling the sun on her skin or the warm water of a bath? She can't just put this behind her and move on; she can't move. She may never be able to move again.

"You don't believe everything happens for a reason?" Shirley is clearly surprised.

"Well, I believe that everything is caused, but that's not the same thing as saying that everything happens for a reason. Let me give you an example." I take a breath. "When I was a little younger than you are right now I was raped. The rape was caused by a combination of the choices I made and choices the man made. Don't get me wrong: I'm not letting him off the hook; he was the one who chose to rape me. But I repeatedly ignored my intuition when it told me I was in a dangerous situation. And I learned a lot from this horrible experience: I learned to trust my intuition and act on it, even when others might think I am overreacting; I learned about an inner strength I didn't know I had; I learned how to live with an ache inside that took a long time to go away and still choose life. But do I think these lessons were the reasons the rape occurred—that some force in the universe choreographed the rape so I could learn these lessons? No. I don't."

"Do you believe in God?" Shirley's voice is nonjudgmental, curious, no doubt baffled why anyone with such a New Age–sounding name does not hold one of the beliefs that is fundamental to many New Age philosophies.

"Yes. I experience something larger than myself—what you call God, what I call the Mystery—around and within me every day. And I experience this presence as powerful and loving. And to tell you the truth, if I thought that a powerful, loving presence had decided that the way to teach me to appreciate my strength was to choreograph a rape in my life, I'd be pretty pissed off. Surely such a force, if it was arranging things, could find a way other than rape—or paralysis—to teach us. I don't think the best way to teach even reluctant students is to hit them over the head, and I think we, as human beings, by our nature want to learn how to live and love fully. So I feel pretty certain that a powerful, loving presence would find a way to teach us—if it were choreographing lessons—with loving encouragement, not devastating tragedy. This doesn't mean we can't learn something from everything that happens, just that those lessons are not necessarily the causal reason behind the events."

"So . . ." I can hear Shirley mulling my words. "Why do you think these things happen?"

"Well, if you're talking about what causes any given thing to happen, we can usually trace it back to a combination of choices and physical conditions. Serious car accidents happen because we choose to build our communities and arrange our lives in such a way that necessitates moving very quickly from one place to another, and we choose to do this in vehicles we know won't withstand the inevitable collisions that occur when a number of factors combine. The weather is bad, or an animal jumps out onto the road, or a piece of metal or rubber wears out, and if these things are combined with someone's choice to drive when he or she is tired or upset or drunk or distracted, there's an accident. We're human beings. We make mistakes. We don't anticipate consequences, or we do but we think the risk is worth it because other things, like profit or the pleasure of the moment, seem more important."

"But do you think there's ever a bigger reason, a higher purpose?"

"I don't know. I don't think we can know if there is a bigger reason—an intentional purpose—that causes these things. I'm not saying we shouldn't consider the bigger meaning in the patterns of our lives, if we can do that without blame or shame. Multiple car accidents in one family is a reason to pause and consider, 'What's going on here?' There seems to be a pattern." I stop for a moment, reaching for a way to be clear. "I do think that our own unconscious, the collective unconscious, and that which is larger than ourselves can speak to us in symbols. If in dreams, why not in the events of our lives? It was hard to miss when Christopher Reeve had his riding accident. The man everyone knew as Superman—icon of American strength and goodness, symbol of heroic action—was paralyzed. And then we watched the human man, Christopher, deal with his paralysis and discovered a different kind of hero, one who cannot act, one who shows us courage not so much in doing but in being with what is. We can learn a great deal by seeing the meaning the events in our lives hold for us. I just think we need to be careful about jumping from the meaning we draw from events to a claim that this is why these events occurred."

"Why? Why do we need to be careful? Why can't we just say, 'Well, that's why it happened; Christopher Reeve's accident happened because we all needed to learn about a different kind of hero'? It would be easier than trying to live with not knowing."

She's right. It would be easier, and this is not a theoretical question for her. She has to find a way to live with limitations and difficulties that I cannot pretend to comprehend fully.

"Because we can't know it to be true. And I think real healing—healing that lets us hold ourselves and the injured parts of the world in our hearts, healing that teaches us how to live fully—comes from intimacy, from the ability to be with what is no matter how hard. I know that having an explanation for why hard things happen would make them easier, but I just don't see how anyone can claim to really know why they happen."

Shirley is quiet, and I suddenly have an image of the two of us standing at the edge of a cliff, staring into an abyss—the bottomless chasm of not knowing. I know what I am telling her. I am telling her that to live fully is to choose to live falling though this vast emptiness.

When she speaks again Shirley's voice is smaller. I have to strain to hear her. "And how do you live with that?"

"One day at a time." I answer quietly. "Reaching out to feel the presence of that which is larger than myself holding me, asking for help in finding a way to be with the vastness of what I don't know while still choosing life." I pause. "It's not easy." We are both quiet for a moment. "I have a friend, Catherine, who years ago had a brain aneurysm burst. It left her mentally and physically handicapped; it took the life she had away from her. She and I once talked about why this had happened to her, and she said to me, 'We can't know why this happened. All we can do is make it count.' She told me, 'So make it count, Oriah. Make it count.'

"I think what she meant was that we have to learn all we can from everything that happens in our lives and act on that learning and share what we learn with others by how we live. That's how we make everything that happens count. And it's an amazing testament to the human spirit—to who and what we really are—that a great deal of the time this is exactly what people do. They go on, they learn from tragedy and live with their hearts open to life again."

Shirley and I talk for a while longer. I tell her that I would be happy to come and sit with her, hear about her experience, and do some ceremony and meditation with her if this is what she wants. I tell her I will leave it up to her to contact me if she would like to get together.

It has been weeks since I spoke with Shirley. I don't expect her to call, and that's okay. The purpose of our conversation was to be sure she knew what I could and could not offer her. There are lots of teachers and spiritual counselors she can contact who will tell her that her paralysis is just one of the many things that had to happen in her life to teach her what she needed to learn for her spiritual development. And maybe that will help her to go on. Sometimes we all need to believe something we cannot know to be true just to continue. Some days the emptiness of not knowing is just too terrifying.

The automatic human response to emptiness seems to be to try to fill it or at least to reach out and grab something to hang on to as we plummet down through the void. When my elder son, Brendan, was born, he was placed on my belly and covered with a blanket. I held him there next to my skin until the umbilical cord stopped pulsing and was cut. After a while the midwife laid him beside me on the bed to examine him, to make sure the proper number of fingers and toes were all in the right places. It was a hot day in July, the room was warm, and he was laid on a flannel blanket. But the second he was laid down he screamed and frantically flung out both arms, seeking something to hang on to. Physically alone for the first time with only the warm air of the room touching most of his body, he was lost in a vast and unfamiliar emptiness. His tiny red fist reached up and grabbed the only thing in his vicinity—the midwife's long ponytail—and yanked it toward him with amazing strength, pulling her face close to his as if to say, "Don't leave me alone out here in this nothingness. I don't like it!"

This is what it is like for us sometimes in the emptiness—terrifying. And we grab at what is available and pull it close to us. Hopefully we have surrounded ourselves with people and places and ideas and practices that that remind us that we belong, that we are always connected to that which sustains life. Otherwise we are left grabbing for things that may lower our anxiety but do so by removing us from ourselves and the world, anesthetizing our ability to feel pleasure as well as pain. Alcohol, drugs, food, emotional drama, overwork—the possibilities are endless.

I do not face anything like the challenge in Shirley's young life, and yet I find myself at times unable or unwilling to simply be with that emptiness that holds my awareness of what I do not know and much more. For me the hardest time, the time when I reach to fill the emptiness, is in the evening. Sometimes—not always—when all the work that needs to be done is finished, when the computer has been shut down because I know trying to write more will be counterproductive, when the dishes have been washed and put away and preparations for the next day are complete but there is still an hour or two before sleep, sometimes a tiny thread of anxiety seeps out from a small cold knot in my belly and travels down through my legs and up into my throat. It's not a specific worry but a thin, unnameable tension that makes me restless, unable or unwilling to simply sit still. So I decide to update my financial books, or I flip through the channels on the TV, busying my mind with work or images of stories I do not care about until I fall exhausted into sleep.

What is it I fear in those dark quiet hours of emptiness? What we all fear: all the unacknowledged grief and despair we feel might overwhelm us; all the unanswerable doubts and the questions whose answers might challenge us to change how we live our lives; knowledge of our own mortality, the brevity of our own precious life and the vastness of what we do not know.

What we forget is that at the center of it all there waits for us a sacred emptiness, a spaciousness, a stillness that renews and lets us remember who and what we are. But we cannot go around the ache— the grief or despair or doubt or hard knowledge—that lies between us and this sacred center. We have to go through it, be with it if we are to find the vastness of the Mystery. That we so often find ourselves aching for empty time, longing for a sense of spaciousness in our lives, is a testament to our deep knowledge that living with an awareness of this emptiness is a necessary part of living life fully. In the Native American teachings in which I have been trained, we begin our prayers by calling upon and coming into alignment with Wwakwan, Great-Grandmother—the void, the nothingness, the sacred womb from which all things are birthed. Often I call upon the spirit of Wwakwan, asking to experience the spaciousness at the center of my being, my day. I sit in silence and use my imagination to connect with the vast space that is at the center of the very matter of which I am made. I taste the Mystery of form that is emptiness, emptiness that is form, and this opens me to the possibility of finding the pause at the end of the exhale before the impulse to inhale, the quiet, empty spaciousness at the center of a busy day.

To dance—to be who we really are and live true to our soul's desires—we must return again and again to this sacred emptiness because deep within we know, as T. S. Eliot wrote, that:

*Except for the point, the still point*
*There would be no dance*
*and there is only the dance.*

We must find a way—a practice—that can take us to the emptiness and keep us there when we would run from what we fear it holds. Without this our lives become, not the graceful movement that dances awake who we are, but the stumbling sleepwalk or frantic running of those who are afraid because they have forgotten who and what they really are.

A practice is a structured activity that offers us a way to consciously enter and be with the sacred emptiness at the center of our being. It is by definition done on a regular, preferably daily, basis.

The regularity is what makes it a practice. You do it whether you feel like it or not, and not feeling like it—resistance—seems to be a pretty universal human response to doing anything on a regular basis, at least in Western culture. The structure is what makes the regularity possible. It gives us a way—a method or an activity—with a shape that does not depend upon how we are feeling at the moment. While I have heard many who dismiss the use of a daily practice by claiming that their practice is to be awake and mindful in all their daily activi-ties, I have yet to meet anyone who can do this. As human beings, we have the capacity to be fully present in every moment, but what we have not done each day for one hour, we are unlikely to be able to do for the remaining twenty-three. We want to do postgraduate work while we are still in kindergarten.

My practice includes a daily meditation on the twenty-two prayers of the Sacred Pipe ceremony I was taught many years ago. Without this structure, I would have days when my impatience and reluctance to consciously meet and connect with all aspects of the seen and unseen world would reduce this ceremony to one or two quick prayers. My practice also includes silent meditation and writing, both done for set periods of time. These practices are done simply—a mindfulness meditation on the breath and being with what is around and within me and writing whatever comes by keeping the hand that holds the pen moving on the page. For both, the time commitment provides me with a container, a simple structure that keeps me there when the fear or discomfort of meeting myself in the stillness would give me ample excuses to go do something else.

At the heart of any effective practice, whether it is explicitly spiri-tual, inherently creative, or rigorously physical, is a structure that clears and holds open a space and time for slowing down and letting go. Letting go necessitates being with the fear that comes when we become aware that all that we love in the world—our very life itself—is impermanent. It can bring tremendous relief and rest to let go where we are trying to hold on, trying to keep the same those things which by their very nature are constantly changing. This does not mean loving life and the world any less fiercely. Loving well and living fully are not the same as holding on.

But we cannot become conscious of where we are holding on, where we need to let go, without slowing down. While it may be possible theoretically to run through our day doing a hundred tasks while maintaining an inner sense of spacious calm, this once again sounds like premature postgraduate work to me. I need to slow down.

We survive by becoming entrained to the speed around us—by coming into alignment with the world we live in. And we live in a fast world. If we want to create a world that is not perpetually speeding up, families and workplaces and communities that support people in slowing down every day in order to stay in touch with and care for themselves and the world, *we* have to slow down. As Gandhi said, *You have to be the change you want to see in the world*. You cannot speed up your efforts to create a life that is slower paced any more than you can successfully fight for peace.

When we avoid the emptiness, when we fill the stillness with too much doing, we are often trying to outrun our sometimes unconscious conviction that who we are will never be enough. The things we try to hang on to—our work, our relationships, our reputation and perspective—are the things we believe will make us worthy of life and love even though we fear we are basically and inherently flawed. If we can simply be with the fear that we are not enough, and with the vastness of what we do not know, we discover an emptiness that is not our failure but is the very source of the fullness of who and what we are. We discover that who we really are—compassionate, gentle beings capable of being with every moment—has always been enough.

Simple but not easy. Easier if done gently, over time and with others. I did the prayers and meditations of my practice regularly but not daily for over ten years, by myself and within community, before they truly became an integral and accepted part of my time alone each day. And even now there are days, like the day Shirley and I spoke of her accident, when I want to be more than I am, offer more than I have—days when being with the emptiness of all I do not know is hard.

I choose to stay with the emptiness of not knowing why Shirley is paralyzed, why I was raped, or why Catherine had a brain aneurysm. And Shirley, knowing this, surprises me and calls weeks after our initial conversation. She tells me she has thought about what I said and wants me to come and visit her. I am awed by her courage, stunned by this fierce compassion—this ability to open our hearts to ourselves and the world and be *with* what is—that gives her the strength to choose to be with what is hard and still choose life. This is who we are. And it is enough.

I will go and be with her, two women sharing our stories with each other. And if we find a moment when our capacity to truly be together is realized, perhaps we will sit in silence, in the vastness of all we do not know, and find together the sacred emptiness that holds us. This is what I want—to be who and what we really are with each other, to dance together.

*Don't say, "Yes!"*
*Just take my hand and dance with me.*

### *Meditation for Slowing Down and Letting Go*

Sit or lie down in a comfortable position with your eyes closed. Breathe three deep breaths in through your nose and out through your mouth, letting your body relax a little on each exhale. Let your shoulders drop, and allow your weight to be fully supported by the surface beneath you and the earth beneath this surface.

Now bring your attention to your breath, breathing normally. Be aware of the rising of your body on the inhale and the falling of your body on the exhale. Breathe normally, just watching the breath as it enters and leaves your body. If thoughts come, simply acknowledge them and let them slip away with your exhale, each time bringing your attention back to your breath.

Now as you inhale, begin to say to yourself, "Slow down." On each inhale as your body fills with air, hear within yourself the phrase "slow down." Notice without judgment any feelings that come when you hear this phrase. Breathe in these feelings, simply being with them as you repeat the phrase internally with each inhale, "slow down." If specific situations or tasks come to mind, simply acknowledge them and let them go with the exhale, bringing your attention back to your breath and repeating internally on the inhale "slow down."

Now, still using the phrase "slow down" on the inhale, add the phrase "let go" on the exhale. With each full inhale, let yourself hear the words "slow down." And with each full exhale, repeat internally the words "let go." "Slow down" on the inhale, and "let go" on the exhale.

Begin to move your breath throughout your body, beginning with your feet and moving up the body. Breathe into your feet, saying "slow down," and exhale from your feet saying "let go." Let any stress or tension or holding on in your feet release with the exhale. Breathe into your lower legs—first one and then the other—breathing "slow down," into the legs and breathing out "let go" on the exhale. Breathe into your thighs—first one and then the other, "slow down" on the inhale and "let go" on the exhale. Breathe into your abdomen and buttocks, the whole pelvic area, saying "slow down" on the inhale and "let go" on the exhale. Breathe into your lower back and then your upper back, breathing in the slowing down and breathing out the letting go of anything that is held there. Breathe into your chest—into your heart and lungs—on every breath repeating "slow down" on the inhale and "let go" on the exhale. If thoughts and feelings come, simply be with them, acknowledge them, and bring your attention back to your breath and the phrases you are repeating internally. Breathe into your hands and your arms, telling them to "slow down" and "let go." Breathe into your shoulders and neck, and then your face and head, on each breath repeating the phrases "slow down" and "let go."

Where are you afraid to slow down? What are you trying to hang on to? Let yourself see, without judgment, where it is easy or hard for you to slow down and let go, and breathe into your whole body, repeating the phrases on the inhale and exhale.

ACKNOWLEDGMENTS

I offer my heartfelt thanks to those who have enabled me to live my dream of writing: to Joe Durepos, my agent, whose integrity, enthusiasm, and bad jokes keep me open to the possibilities; to the team at Harper San Francisco, who have sent my words out into the world with wonderful support, including publisher Stephen Hanselman, for his vision and commitment; editor John Loudon, for his encouragement and love of the word; and Margery Buchanan, Calla Devlin, Kris Ashley, Priscilla Stuckey, Lisa Zuniga, Jim Warner, and Donna Marie Grethen, for the many talents they have brought to the creation of *The Dance*.

I have been blessed to receive guidance and support from many whose advice and example have guided me and whose humor has reminded me not to take myself too seriously. These generous souls include Ellen Wingard, Gail Straub, Mark Kelso, Elizabeth Lesser, Greg Zelonka, Cheryl Richardson, Jon Kabat-Zinn, Mickey Lemle, John O'Donohue, Wayne Dyer, and Ann Petrie. I continue to be grateful to Peter and Judy Crawford Smith for hosting my retreats—both personal and communal—with impeccable organization and openhearted generosity. In addition, I am grateful to those whose skillful choreography at conferences has allowed me to meet new communities feeling held by their caregiving: Stephan Rechtschaffen, Harry Feinberg, Peter Hogan, and Paul Calens of the Omega

Institute; Robin and Cody Johnson of the Prophets conferences; Karen Thomas of the Mile Hi Church in Denver; and Jan Marie Dore of the International Coach Federation. To these and the many men and women who have shared their stories with me at conferences and retreats, through letters and e-mails, thank you.

Closer to home, I am grateful for the constant resourcefulness and efficient good humor of my assistant and friend, Elizabeth Verwey, and the ongoing generosity of a supportive community that includes Linda Mulhall, Lise Tetrault, Jude Cockman, Cat Scoular, Vivian Taylor Cvetkovic, Philomene Hoffman, Judith Edwards, Peter Marmorek, Catherine Mloszewska, Liza Parkinson, Diana Meredith, Teri Degler, Wilder Penfield, Nancy Ross, Carla Jensen, Joseph Lukezich, Christina Vander Pyl, Ellen Martin, Mark Dreu, and Ingrid Szymkowiak.

And always there are the voices of love and support from my sons, Brendan and Nathan, and my parents, Don and Carolyn House. I am so grateful for the family I have. And thank you, Jeff—for finding me, for loving me still after thirty years of absence, for truly being with me.

Last, I offer a prayer of gratitude to that presence that is larger than myself and never fails to hold me in its compassionate heart. I am grateful to know the touch of this Mystery in my life.

For information about Oriah Mountain Dreamer's retreats and speaking schedule:

Go to: www.oriahmountaindreamer.com

Or write:
300 Coxwell Avenue
Box 22546
Toronto, ON
M4L 2A0
Canada

# The Invitation

## ORIAH MOUNTAIN DREAMER

*Experience the challenge that is changing lives everywhere!*

'The Invitation' is a poem that has been distributed worldwide. It has created a sensation and sparked this book that works with the poem's elements and ideas in a step by step guidebook.

When workshop leader and author Oriah Mountain Dreamer wrote her heartfelt 'Invitation' a couple of years ago she did not expect this small prose poem to reach the level of popularity that it has. Spread far and wide by word of mouth and the Internet, it has also been read aloud at weddings, funerals and spiritual gatherings by people including Robert Bly and Jack Cornfield.

The poem is a challenge to us and in this accessible and inspiring book Oriah Mountain Dreamer tells us how to meet that challenge.

Oriah Mountain Dreamer leads spirituality workshops throughout Canada and the US and lives in Toronto.

ISBN 0 7225 4045 0
Order now at www.thorsons.com